with best

Versed in Medicine

Versed in Medicine

George Morrison Jolly

Jeremy Mudditt
Publishing Services

First published 2000 on behalf of the author
by Jeremy Mudditt Publishing Services
3 Longlands Road, Carlisle,
Cumbria, CA3 9AD, UK

04 03 02 01 00 7 6 5 4 3 2 1

British Library Cataloguing in Publication Data
A catalogue record for this book is available from the British Library.

ISBN 1-902621-01-8

Typeset by Reesprint, Radley, Oxfordshire, OX14 3AJ

Printed and bound in Great Britain by
Campsie Print Group, Glasgow, G40 4EH

I have eaten your bread and salt
   I have drunk your water and wine
The deaths ye died I have watched beside
   And the lives ye led were mine.
Was there aught that I did not share
   Of vigil or toil or ease
One joy or woe that I did not know
   Dear hearts across the seas?
I have written the tale of our lives
   For a sheltered people's mirth
In jesting guise but ye are wise
   And ye know what the jest is worth.

Rudyard Kipling

Contents

List of Illustrations

Acknowledgements

To my mother, who gave me my love of lyric poetry, and with her Highland second sight foresaw that I would write.

To my father who passed on to me a good memory and what brain I have.

To my Editor, Christine Orme, whose meticulous revising and suggestion have reminded me of the animal who said that the worst of being a hog was that people were too often trying to make a silk purse out of your wife's ear!

And lastly, to the citizens of Carlisle, capital city of the fairest county in England, my thanks in verse:

In a pleasant land of hawthorn and hydrangea
  Never far away from mountain and the sea
Stands a city sometimes doubtful of the stranger
  But found it in her heart to welcome me.

And now as round me all the shadows lengthen
  I close my eyes for just a moment while
Momentarily I feel an inner strength when
  I thank providence and the burghers of Carlisle.

CHAPTER ONE

Bairn and Schoolboy: Scotland and India

An icy blast o' Januar wind blew Hansel in on Robin.

So wrote Burns, as celebrants of his birthday the world over will recall. Though I was born at a different season – on 1 June – the blast that welcomed me in Edinburgh, my native city, could well have been equally cold, Edinburgh being the city it is of 'blown grey spaces'. I was to remain among those blown grey spaces almost continuously until my graduation in 1938. Although I was a ten-pound baby, this early promise was never fulfilled and I reached just under 5' 6" in my young prime. It's never bothered me too much, since though it may have disadvantaged me in competition for the ladies, on the plus side are the facts that I didn't bang my head on low beams and – touch wood – have not been susceptible to back trouble, unlike my taller brethren.

On the distaff side my ancestry is Highland. My Gaelic-speaking mother, Katharine Isabella (known to her family as Katie Belle) was a McKenzie of the clan Seaforth, whose father, Murdo Morrison, ran a fishing fleet in Stornaway where she was brought up. By contrast my father, after whom I was named, was a Lowland Scot, the third son of the minister of Edinburgh's Westport church set at the ancient

West Gate of the city, scene of much fierce fighting in the old bloodthirsty days.

My paternal grandfather, James, whom I never knew, died relatively young, leaving seven children, no money, and, curiously among that generation, no knowledge of his origins. So my grandmother was widowed early, but her family were well-educated by the Church of Scotland, as ever looking after its own, and her late husband would have been proud of them had he lived. The eldest son, Jack, became a senior civil servant in the Admiralty, the second, Willie, Professor of Physiology at the University of Cape Town, the third, my father George, a Lieutenant-Colonel in the Indian Medical Service and a gifted artist and linguist, whilst the youngest, Gordon, always regarded as the 'thickest' of the family, also ended up in the Indian Medical Service – as Director General, retiring with the rank of Lieutenant-General and a knighthood! The three girls, Grace, Mary and Eva, all had pictures hung in the Scottish Academy.

As some might guess, my family name is of French origin. My father's ancestors were Huguenots – French Protestants – mostly weavers, living in the region of La Rochelle on the west coast of France. In 1585 thousands of Huguenots were forced to flee France when King Henry of Navarre, also a Protestant, was compelled to change his faith. The massacre of St Bartholomew's Eve followed, and the Huguenots holed up in groups throughout western Europe, from the Orkneys to the Low Countries. In actual fact, I am probably of French stock on both sides, as my mother's family has been traced back to King Robert the Bruce, who was of course Norman – Robert de Bruce, so, to quote Burns again:

> My ancient and ignoble blood
> has flowed through scoundrels since the flood.

Even before I was born, periodic displacement was to be the norm. My mother, the aforementioned Katie Belle, retained both her sense of humour and her love of poetry despite trauma and hardship and lived to be 91. She was an indomitable little lady, as witness the fact that in 1911 she had travelled home alone from Japan on the Trans-Siberian railway, whilst pregnant with my sister. Since my father was one of the few Europeans then who spoke Japanese, and, even more rarely, wrote it, he had been seconded to Japan in an intelligence role, and he and my mother lived there for three years soon after their marriage. They considered Japanese women delightful (though that is not an adjective they used so freely about the men) and the Japanese countryside enchanted them. My sister was conceived in Japan at a time when the wistaria was in full bloom and very beautiful. As a direct consequence of this my parents christened her Wistaria, a name which was not, in later life, a source of unalloyed pleasure to her – so her friends called her Wisty. Four years after my mother's solo trip from Japan she accomplished a similar feat, managing somehow in 1915, in the middle of the Great War, to get herself home from India alone, to have me!

Once I was safely born, my mother wished to rejoin her husband in India, but as it was wartime, there was no possibility of her obtaining passages for me or my sister. My mother's older sister, Chrissie, married but childless and living in Sutton Coldfield, nobly volunteered to have us, and for the next three years just as nobly cared for us. It was, I suspect, as much a wrench for her as it was for us when our mother returned at the end of the war, to be greeted as a stranger, and moved us back to Edinburgh. My first clear memory is, perhaps not surprisingly, connected with the end of the war – I can recall waving a Union Jack in the garden of my aunt's home in Sutton Coldfield on Armistice Day – 11 November 1918. I was then almost three and a half years old.

Back in Edinburgh, I was sent to the kindergarten of St Brides, the school attended by my sister, my elder by four years. Here I had to wear a round black felt hat, a circumstance which strongly prejudiced me against all forms of headgear, and I have never worn a hat since, except in the Army, where it was obligatory. St Bride's was unremarkable but for the fact that the deputy headmistress, Miss Elsie Lee, left to found another school in Edinburgh, which she named St Trinian's and which in due time became the prototype for Ronald Searle's cartoons and for the film series starring Margaret Rutherford, Alistair Sim and Joyce Grenfell, all of them comedy hits of the time.

About a year and a half after the end of hostilities, my mother managed to obtain passages to India for herself and me. My sister was left behind at school as a boarder, while my mother and I travelled out on *The Victorian*, a ship equipped with less than adequate cold storage for the eastern run. I learned later that a number of babies died on the voyage in consequence of food poisoning, so I was perhaps then, as once or twice since, a lucky survivor. One of my more vivid memories of the voyage out is of being awakened in the upper bunk every morning by an arm appearing at my head, through the window from the passage, and depositing a banana on my chest. The arm in question belonged to a kindly-disposed steward named Skinner.

Another memory from that voyage is of going ashore in Port Said and sitting in a café. A 'gilli-gilli' man came up to the table, placed on it his closed fist and in a moment a live chicken was running about! He put two hands on the chicken and it appeared to divide so that there were two chickens and presently there might be half a dozen of them – fascinating stuff to a five-year-old! These 'gilli-gilli' men met the ships for many years – I wonder if they still do? Landing at Bombay in due course I made my very first acquaintance with my father.

Until that landing in Bombay, my father and I had never met. Seventy-nine years on I cannot put my hand on my heart and say how he looked to me, because I have absolutely no recollection of that first meeting. However, later memories are of a smallish man, sometimes in uniform, who usually came into my bedroom just before I went to sleep and read to me verses from Omar Khayyam. I had no idea what they meant, but the sound of them fascinated me, and I could still repeat them to you verbatim if you were unwise enough ever to ask me. I remember too my father's very clever sketches and caricatures of our Indian companions – he was a gifted artist and had wished to pursue art rather than medicine as a career, but convention then forbade such a course. He was, I recall, a gentle man with a very quick wit (though I do remember once seeing him in a towering rage, when he came upon our cook straining the soup through his socks!) but he was also frail, a result of long service and successive illnesses in an unfriendly climate.

An officer such as my father in the Indian Medical Service tended to have wide responsibilities. Very often he would be the only non-Indian doctor in a large town. My father, and others in his situation elsewhere, took command of the hospital, did major surgery, trained his juniors, was responsible for public health, looked after the European community and also, in my father's case, the medical needs of the jail which happened to be close to our house. (It was odd at first to have prisoners with leg irons working in our garden, but I soon got used to and made friends with them.) I can remember witnessing from a window a beating in the jail courtyard, no one having realised I was there, and on another occasion I might have witnessed a hanging, but someone found me in time. Perhaps I would have needed counselling.

My father was Civil Surgeon in Benares, now known as Varanesi, the sacred city of the Hindus where they gather annually from all over the subcontinent to burn their dead beside the holy River Ganges. To this day I can still visualise Benares railway station with corpses wrapped like mummies as far as the eye could see, and I remember watching the bodies being burned on the banks of the river, the bearers chanting to the god Rama.

> Call on Rama, going slowly
> As ye bear a brother lowly.
> He may hear and he may heed
> Perchance your voice.

The population of this city sacred to Rama could swell overnight from a third of a million to a million. Problems of public health there would have driven those who administer our Health Service now right 'off their trolleys'!

As I remember it from a child's perspective, it was a great life. The British Raj was still securely based and even officers not very high up in the pecking order had at least a dozen servants, who were paid only a pittance no doubt, but got their keep at least. I still remember with affection our servants – Nazir Khan, the bearer or valet who managed the household, Abdul Hai, the *khitmagar*, or butler, the *khansama* (cook), the *mali* (gardener), *dhobi* (laundryman), *chaprassi* (messenger), *chowkidar* (night watchman) and ayah (nanny) as well as a grasscutter and syce who dealt with the horses and, by that time, a chauffeur – Gulab Mohammed.

To keep these numerous servants employed and in an attempt to direct one's thoughts away from some of the more uncomfortable and dangerous realities of life, dinner parties were frequent amongst expatriates in India. The social life for a little boy was good – he couldn't be left alone in the bungalow at night, so when there wasn't a dinner party, he went along to the Club with his elders. The downside of this however was that, with so much adult company, he was in danger of becoming a precocious little prig, a condition which was rapidly sorted out when he went back to school in the UK!

In each cantonment or European community in India, there operated a caste system as rigid as any in the Hindu world. At the top of the heap was the Commissioner with his lady; the Commissioner was the senior officer present of the Indian Civil Service. Then came the Judge, next the Collector, the senior finance man, and below them service personnel, then the police, the railway and – down at the bottom – the missionaries. This rigid caste-system applied at all times, so when 'Greek met Greek' in the Club at night, snobbery was the rule:

> And this is the city of Boston
>   The home of the bean and the cod
> Where Lowells talk just to the Cabots
>   And the Cabots talk only to God.

Nobody who has lived in the East can ever forget the experience – the sights, the sounds, and especially the smells, which even today, years later, can evoke the most vivid memories. Indian smells were and still are, memorable. I am sometimes even now reminded of the smell of an Indian village at evening when cooking fires are stoked with cow dung – not an unpleasant smell, strangely enough, but sickly sweet. I remember too the pungently-inviting smells of the bazaars in India – very much off-limits to a little boy because they contained *germs*!

Of my abiding memories of India, the most vivid I think is of seeing the Taj Mahal by moonlight, that wonderful memorial which Shah Jehan built to commemorate his wife Mumtazi Mahal. He had intended a corresponding mausoleum in black marble on the other side of the river for himself but his wishes were never fulfilled. Another memory is of being left by my father – who was visiting an outlying Maharajah – in, of all places, the harem for an hour and a half. I looked and wondered, but some faint instinctive stirring inside suggested I should be doing more.

The summer heat in the city was well-nigh unbearable so those Europeans who could do so went up to the Hill-Station of Mussoorie where it was cooler. Here on one occasion I fell down a flight of stone steps and broke my right arm. It was a bad break and I had to be carried about 6,000 feet down the mountainside to the Military Station of Dehra Dun for an X-ray. I was transported in a *dhoolie*, a kind of stretcher with a sun-canopy on it, and by the time I was carried back I was delirious, but I still remember the gentleness and kindness of the Indians who dealt with me and handled me on that occasion. Had the partition of India not come when it did in 1947, I believe I too could have served in the Indian Medical Service, as I loved the Indians.

Whilst I thrived and loved India – not least the Indians themselves – my father's health was deteriorating rapidly owing to illness and the demands of his career. He spent 25 years altogether in the East during which time he suffered most of the illnesses that were so prevalent out there, mostly serious.

My mother and I returned from India in 1924 in the P&O liner *Kaiser i Hind* – a pleasant voyage, on which, I believe, I first acquired a taste for alcohol. I would be put to bed in the upper berth and, when my mother came to dress for dinner, she brought with her from the bar a glass of her favourite dry vermouth which she set on the dressing table while she went to the bathroom. I had a tiny bucket which I would lower from above and skilfully drain off about a quarter of the drink. I enjoyed that six-week voyage! On this trip we went ashore at Aden, which was dusty and squalid, but passing through the Suez canal by moonlight I saw wonderful silhouettes of camels.

Some passengers disembarked at Marseilles to travel overland across France, cutting out quite a lot of mileage and the Bay of Biscay, which gave us rather a hot reception, but we arrived safely and eventually there was an affectionate reunion with my sister in Edinburgh, where we lived in a flat, as many do. When shortly after this my father was invalided out of the Indian Medical Service, we were together as a family for the first time!

I was eight years old and my sister about twelve when we returned to Edinburgh. Understandably, after living for several years in India, I thought Edinburgh the cold place that it indeed is, but I seemed to thrive pretty well. I was sent to George Watson's College, part day-school and part boarding, which now proclaims itself the largest independent school in Britain, whatever that may mean. George Watson's had a tradition of producing doctors and also statesmen. During the first war it had supplied two members of the War Cabinet, and since then two Home Secretaries – Sir David Maxwell Fyfe and Sir John Anderson, who gave wartime Britain the Anderson Shelter. More recently Sir Malcolm Rifkind, another old boy of George Watson's, was Foreign Secretary.

In my day, though regarded as a fringe public school, it was more day-school than boarding and I lived at home, taking the long tram ride there and back across Edinburgh alone

– the world was a safer place for children then. The postwar food shortages were probably over as I have no recollection of feeling hungry on my bowl of soup (price one old penny) and sandwiches at lunchtime. I don't think I went to school in India – certainly I have no memory of so doing, my education on the sub-continent being entrusted to the hands of sundry well-disposed ladies as we moved about a good deal. Despite this I took well to a large school, having always been a gregarious animal, and Scottish education has a good tradition from the village school upwards. As my readers will know, when the Angles landed in Northumbria in the fifth century, the acute Angles turned north and became Scots, while the obtuse Angles … well perhaps I can leave you to work out what happened to them!

As I said earlier, periodic displacement was the norm for me, and we had been back in Edinburgh for only a couple of years when my father bought a practice in Kirkwall, Orkney and my parents and I moved there, leaving my sister once again at her boarding-school, St Brides, in Edinburgh. I was by now about ten years old and spent a year at the local high school, but sadly my father's health broke down and he didn't work again so we returned to Edinburgh and I to Watson's – further on academically than the classmates I rejoined: Kirkwall School has a high standard of education and Orcadians are clever people. As a bonus from a year in Orkney I had at my fingertips the facts of life which had been tactfully and carefully kept from me in India.

Though remote, there was nothing primitive about Kirkwall; in fact it was the first town in Britain to be lit by electricity. Sir Walter Scott had written his novel *The Pirate* (published in 1821) in 'Skerryvore' the big, spooky house standing at one end of the main street, in which we lived in Kirkwall. It faced St Magnus Cathedral, in magnificent repair and worth a visit any time. I used to play marbles in the forecourt. I have to confess that I was a bit young to read Scott's novel when we lived there, and I haven't done so since, but I understand that *The Pirate* is set mainly in Shetland, so perhaps Scott lived in Kirkwall to gain local knowledge as a background for the book.

Orkney and Shetland are fascinating places full of history, with many Pictish dwellings and other antiquities well worth a visit. The islands are almost bare of trees and the wind is a frequent visitor; nonetheless, Orkney is a prosperous agricultural community and distils my favourite Malt whiskey – Highland Park.

P&O have a selection of very pleasant cruises to the islands from either Leith or Aberdeen. I took one back to Kirkwall when I was in my late thirties, accompanied by my wife Hazel, and sought out my former nursemaid who had accompanied us from Edinburgh to Kirkwall and who had remained there and married a farmer. She was a good deal more prosperous than I was! Although we were there for only one full day, by the time we left on the ship at 8 o'clock at night she had assembled about half a dozen of my old classmates from my year in Kirkwall to see us off. It was like *This is Your Life* in miniature. Among them was my closest friend George Finlay, who was known at school as Pedy Plowty (*pedy* is an Orcadian word meaning little, which must, I think, derive from the French, *petit*). He was by that time the Yachting Correspondent of The Glasgow Herald.

Back at Watson's my schooldays were not over-distinguished. I played rugby and, rather more effectively, golf. In my last year, along with three others I had my prefect's badge removed for a week for a misdemeanour which I shall not enlarge upon here. We were all destined for Medicine. The Headmaster, when he carpeted us and made his thoughts known, said that no boys who had behaved as we had done could expect to make any success of their chosen vocations. In the event, one, Morris Carstairs, became Professor of Psychiatry at York and eventually Vice-Chancellor, and gave the BBC Reith Lectures. The second, John MacLeod, ended up as Senior Reader in Medicine at Edinburgh University, whilst the third, Douglas Robertson, nicknamed Fessie from his professorial appearance, became Senior Medical Officer at Unilever. Of the four of us, I was the only one who fell off the ladder and became a GP. One out of four was not good forecasting for the late George Robertson MA.

I left school with a Bursary but not a particularly good one. Had I followed my own bent I would have gone in for English, by far my strongest interest and strongest subject. I was put off this, however, by the thought that I would probably end up teaching it. I never reckoned myself cut out to be a successful teacher so I followed a number of friends and a family tradition into medicine. My son, Hugh, was later to follow me. It didn't occur to me to go to any other Medical School but Edinburgh: my father and his youngest brother Gordon had both done Medicine there and, when I started the course, my father was in poor health. By remaining at home I could share his care with my mother. I was very content to stay a citizen of High Dunedin (the old name for Edinburgh) until my Graduation.

I don't believe my sights were ever too high. I had neither a scientific nor a mathematical mind nor too much manual dexterity, and was in fact always more interested in the mind than the body. I have since realised that medical graduates split naturally into two categories – those who are going to deal with people and those who are going to deal with microscopes or statistics – or for that matter students. I think one senses at quite an early stage in which category one is going to function for the rest of one's life.

I had no ambition beyond General Practice and looking back I have no regrets. It was, and still is, a hard and sometimes worrying life but it can be very worthwhile. The plus side is the willingness of patients to integrate you into their families literally from the cradle to the grave and that can be very rewarding.

A little later in my life when I came out of the Army, I could perhaps have trained as a psychiatrist, but by that time I had a wife and child to support and required the wherewithal quickly, so the choice was really made for me.

CHAPTER TWO

The Cloisters of Academe

My career at Edinburgh University reading Medicine was as middle-of-the-road as my schooldays had been. Medical training in my day was stereotyped: in the first year we studied Chemistry, Physics, Botany, Zoology and Anatomy. I failed Botany and had to re-sit the exam, but have ever since turned that failure to good account by using it to my wife as a reason why I shouldn't be expected to garden – obviously I am not to be trusted with plants!

Second-year subjects were Anatomy and Physiology, and in the third, in addition to Pathology and Pharmacology, we were let loose on medical and surgical wards. The fourth year witnessed an introduction to Forensic Medicine, Public Health and Obstetrics and Gynaecology, whilst in the fifth we did much more work in Clinics.

I imagine that, sixty years on, things are now very different: advances in antisepsis and the use of disposable equipment will have made life better for medical students, and the advent of antibiotics will have ensured that students do not now have to watch slow deaths that no one can prevent.

Edinburgh Medical School has always produced great men and my time saw a flowering of these, including some whose giftedness was matched only by their eccentricity. The most eye-catching was the Professor of Obstetrics,

R. W. Johnstone, whose surname was pronounced as in the two words – John Stone. The last of the Victorians, Professor Johnstone – wearing top hat and morning coat – would arrive in state at the Infirmary to be ushered from his Rolls by his chauffeur. He did at least take off the top hat and morning coat when he operated. His sights were always high. He once remarked to us during a lecture, 'I remember with what a mixture of awe and of pleasure I first gazed on the perineum of a duchess.' (Like, I thought to myself, *stout Cortez* in Keats's poem):

> … when with eagle eyes
> he gazed at the Pacific – and all his men
> Looked at each other with a wild surmise –
> Silent upon a peak in Darien.[1]

In sharp contrast, 'Pussy' Stewart, Consultant Surgeon, was helped onto his bicycle by his house surgeon at the end of his operating list. Pussy, a religious man, could sometimes be observed pre-operatively kneeling to pray for strength – as the surgeons did in pre-anaesthetic days, to do the terrible things that they had to do.

Surgeons were always the most colourful. In those days, when half the country's Royalty had sacrificed their lives to cigarettes, if you were a medic and didn't smoke, people regarded you as an oddity. I remember Frankie Jardine, a skilled surgeon and chain-smoker coming in to scrub up: the last thing he did after finishing scrubbing up was spit the stump between his lips into the sink. Smoking being the norm in those days, it must have been hard for non-smokers: I recall Todd, an irascible physician who, his initials being T.R.R., was inevitably known as Tarara. He would enter a

1 (Sonnets: *On First Looking into Chapman's Homer*)

lecture theatre where most of his audience had been smoking and give his lecture with all the disgust of a non-smoker visible on his countenance throughout.

Another memorable figure was a Professor of Medicine – Derrick (later *Sir* Derrick) Dunlop. He had dark, flowing locks, a slight lisp and the looks of an Adonis with the result that his lady patients were rapt with ecstasy in his presence. We students were equally his slaves, since it was most unusual for us to be treated with anything but disdain by these demi-gods. When you became a doctor, you acquired slight prestige, but a medical student is the lowest form of hospital life.

The doyen of them all, however, was Sir John Frazer, Baronet, a Churchillian figure mentally and physically, who always used the royal 'we' when lecturing. His theatre would be filled with up to 300 devotees from all over the world, who came to see him do his Outpatients. If you were unlucky enough to be called out from your seat as a student to make an examination, you had the full gaze of publicity on you. I remember one student who, having been summoned by the great man to examine a breast, was thankfully regaining his seat only to be told, 'Now do it again, Mr So-and-So – and this time do it medically, not socially'!

Lectures in pathology, an unexciting subject except to the devotee, took place immediately after lunch in a darkened lecture theatre with slides. The audience fell into three categories. Those in the front rows were the bright stars of the future, those in the middle rows probably asleep and those in the back had probably lit cigarettes. From where Professor Drennan stood and lectured it must have looked like a swarm of fireflies. Every so often a sudden 'lights on' was tried but it always proved impossible to identify the culprits so perhaps the practice continues to this day. Professor Drennan's son was in my year, and I was destined to meet him in later life in different circumstances, as I shall recount in due course.

Edinburgh surgeons, it would seem, are strong men and resourceful too. Many years ago in the national press I came across this story. Bruce Clarke FRCS was travelling by rail from Edinburgh, Waverley, to London, Kings Cross. (These were the days when railway compartments were much smaller and held only about six people). He was anxious to sleep but two ladies kept up an incessant conversation, one with a particularly loud voice. Eventually, unable to stand it any longer, he leaned across and without any fuss dislocated the jaw of the more strident lady. This status quo obtained until somewhere in the Home Counties, when he leaned over again and replaced the displaced jaw. There is no record of any aftermath to this. Litigation was something of a rarity in those days.

Incidentally, you might not have heard this not very kind classification of four of the medical specialities:
Neurologist – knows everything and does nothing.
Surgeon – knows nothing and does everything.
Psychiatrist – knows nothing and does nothing.
Pathologist – knows everything but it's too late then anyway.

As for Gynaecologists, or Guineacologists as we Scots with our sense of realism pronounce them, I don't know any definitions but I do know this story: a man went into a London Labour Exchange in search of work and asked, 'Anything for me? The Manager replied, 'I've only one vacancy at present; it's for a Gynaecologist.'

'What's that?'

'Well, I'm not rightly sure but, well, he does things to women.'

'I might as well apply. When?'

'Tomorrow morning – 10 o'clock.'

'I'll be in the office at 10 o'clock.'

'Not much good I'm afraid; the queue starts at Luton.'

In our fourth year we moved closer to nature and did Obstetrics, a process during which we learned as much about humanity as we did about Obstetrics. From Edinburgh Medical School, the richer students went to Dublin and the Rotunda Hospital, which confined itself to Obstetrics. It had a Master and a very good name for teaching, as well as a plentiful supply of babies, but, it being further away, and across the sea, not all of us could afford to go to there. The practical alternative was Glasgow, so to Glasgow we poorer students repaired.

We were required to deliver on district our quota of a dozen babies. We went in pairs, and I was partnered by my friend John Rutherford, who was later to win the MC as a parachute doctor badly wounded at Arnhem. In most other places a nurse accompanied students, but not in Glasgow. I always thought it a most traumatic experience for a young mother at the most vulnerable moment of her life to have to commit herself to two scruffy, ignorant medical students.

Our target, as I've mentioned, was twelve babies, and unless the delivery was done by our own hands in their home it didn't count. We could not proceed further with our medical studies until we had between us brought into the world a dozen babies. It was impossible to forecast how long the entire stint would take. Some were lucky and clicked for mostly multiparous births, that is to say, when the mother had previously given birth to several other babies. Often such mothers delivered later babies quite quickly, sometimes too quickly – remember, they didn't count towards our total if they had been born two seconds before we entered the home! In such cases we just had to grit our teeth and clean up.

Alternatively, we might have to spend up to 24 hours in the house, waiting for some action. In a few of the houses, if we needed to sleep, it had to be in a chair that was not upholstered, lest we should take aboard parasites. Realistically, the only safe way to sleep was in a wooden chair, not too close to the walls (because creepy-crawlies could drop from those!), resting our heads on a scrubbed kitchen table. Only then could we hope to leave the house without any honorary members! Even so, I remember getting into the bath nightly at the midwifery hostel where we were based, and watching the dense black carpet of fleas rising to the surface of the water. It just bore out the old couplet:

> Big fleas have little fleas upon their backs to bite 'em
> And these again have smaller fleas, and so *ad infinitum*.

Even if we were not called out, sleep was not always easy in the midwifery hostel, since it was situated next door to a brothel, the patrons of which would queue noisily on the pavement outside right round the clock. However, since we had to go and revisit daily those whom we had delivered, and advise the mother, there was little time for immoral living!

Our hospital base in Glasgow was the Rotten Row Maternity Hospital, and I remember well the Sister-in-Charge on the Labour Ward there, who was only about five feet high, but always got her baby. If the muscular power of the mother were lacking, Sister would take off her shoes, mount the bed and push with the soles of her feet on the dome of the womb to assist the contractions. If these were lacking altogether, she would walk briskly backwards and forwards across the bare abdomen to start them – a very effective therapy!

Calls came very regularly into the Maternity Hospital, brought usually by the father who travelled by tram. The rules stated clearly that the baby had to be delivered personally. Since the journey there and back by tram was anything but 'a flying squad', it often happened that we got there to find that the baby had already arrived and was lying, wrapped in newspaper, in front of the fire. This didn't count of course and we had to do all the cleaning up and begin all over again, arguing once more with another father about who would pay the tram fares. It was thus very much in the lap of the gods as to how quickly we achieved our target of twelve babies, and how well or otherwise the little beggars behaved themselves on the way out. By the end, we didn't have too starry-eyed a view of babies, I assure you. When the final one had been delivered, we returned post haste to Edinburgh, but then had to travel daily to Glasgow for follow-up visits.

Our series of deliveries yielded one rarity, an anencephalic (literally headless) monster. In fact, it wasn't quite headless, its face being no more than an inch in length. No one seemed too much concerned and on our visit on the third day to check up we found that the baby was still being exhibited and that the neighbours were in the house – not exactly admiring, but eating banana sandwiches which we joined in with pleasure. Very few doctors are privileged to see an anencaphalic –and privileged is the word, for in my entire medical career I have never seen another.

In recent years Glasgow has earned the accolade, 'Culture City of Europe', but we somehow missed that side of it! We never had our noses far beyond the tenements, which were ubiquitous. These varied from those like the infamous Gorbals, ancient and of a pattern, lit by open gas jets and with one communal toilet on each floor, to more modern tenements in the suburbs further out, which had marginally more amenities but were still sadly lacking by modern standards. Those were the days when the denizens of these primitive dwellings used to try to distance themselves from sad reality by indulging in a sort of drug culture, drinking methylated spirits or wood alcohol, or holding a glass of milk under the gas jet in the tenement vestibule to create a narcotic known as stairhead gas.

Glasgow was then a city of gangs, and we had to walk past them as they assembled in the Gorbals or Bridgeton Cross but if we were carrying the magic black bag, they knew who we were and didn't touch us. It would doubtless be very different now in this drug-ridden age. As I said earlier, we learned far more than mere Obstetrics during our time in Glasgow. We discovered, for example, how a minority of families could and did keep a clean house in those dark satanic tenements with their gas jets and communal lavatories. Those few were a triumph for the human spirit! They were generous too – it used to be said of the citizens of Glasgow that if you went into a house of theirs they would say, 'You'll have your tea', whereas if you went into a house in Edinburgh, they would say, 'You'll have had your tea.' I concur!

Edinburgh was our base for the abnormal maternity cases which we also had to do in our fourth year, and for this we moved for two or three weeks at a time into a hostel in Chalmers Street round the corner from the Simpson Memorial Maternity Hospital, J.Y. Simpson being the man who discovered chloroform in Edinburgh. In the hostel was a very colourful redheaded maid whom we knew as Ginger, who brightened our lives. Ginger, I recall, used to come into our bedroom at an early hour and say to me, 'Help me, God Almighty, Mr Jolly – are ye no' out o' your bloody bed yet? Where were you last night – out with your pusher I suppose? Your eyes look like glessy bools this morning.' (Glessy bools in the Scots vernacular are those types of glass marbles with very colourful centres.)

I was sharing a room with a schoolfriend of mine, Bill Russell, son of the Reverend Oliver Russell, to whom he used to refer, not very reverently, as Olly. Olly, like his son, was tall and slim and a lady's man. In due course Bill became a gynaecologist in Cape Town, and also, in due course, my best man. This came about because I was married in Belfast in 1941, and the Army had very conveniently stationed Bill there at that particular time. But all that was several years ahead of us – first we had Finals to get through.

The final year of the medical course is a time when students try to sort into some kind of coherent whole in their minds the amorphous mass of knowledge that has been instilled there under pressure, so that in due course they may delude the examiners into reluctantly accepting that they are fit to be trusted with the power of life and death over their fellows.

My Finals fell in the summer of 1938; they were long drawn-out affairs, taking, I seem to remember, at least a fortnight. The subjects for the examination were Medicine, Surgery, Obstetrics and Gynaecology, although in theory the examiners were entitled to set questions on anything in the entire five-year course. This was always slightly alarming, but for the most part they stuck to the subjects mentioned above.

The exams were divided into three parts, written, oral and practical. The practical exam consisted of patients whom we had to examine and diagnose without, of course, having access to their case notes. Sometimes a whisper from a passing houseman who might have been in our position a year earlier could make a world of difference, as it was largely a matter of luck whether you got a straightforward case or a more abstruse one. For the oral exam, one dressed in one's best bib and tucker and was scrupulously polite to the demi-god who was examining one. The whole process, drawn out as it was, was a considerable ordeal, especially in view of all that hung on the outcome! The results were posted three weeks later, in the June of 1938. In the next year the Second World War was to break out, but I don't think any of us suspected this for a moment.

Fortunately for me this summer of 1938 was tempered with golf. I had played golf for the University for four years, and we were lucky enough to play our inter-university matches at Muirfield. Shortly before my medical Finals we played Yale, who were touring and who numbered the then British Champion, Charley Yates in their ranks. We were well beaten but the match stays in my memory.

I was playing in the foursomes with Joe Menzies, later to be my partner in General Practice. He played near the top of the team, I near the bottom, but we joined up in foursomes. We had both managed to win our morning singles and in the afternoon on that famous last green, I was faced with the need to loft a stymie to keep the match square. (These were the bad old days when the stymie was still a part of the tactics of match-playing.) Since very few of you know, or will ever have played, a stymie I would explain that part of the tactics of playing a match then was, if you didn't hole your putt then you tried to leave your ball between the opponent's ball and the hole when they came to putt. So, if in fact you were laid a stymie by the opposition, you had several options, but the commonest was either to take a lofted club, probably in those days a mashieniblick, pitch the ball over the opposition ball and either straight into the hole, or let it run into the hole like a putt. This was tricky but possibly not as tricky as it might sound. On this occasion, and by the grace of God, I managed it. After that stymie, the Final Exams were almost an anti-climax!

Incidentally, thirty-one years later, when my son Hugh was in the middle of sitting his Finals, I played him in the first round of our club championship in Carlisle and owing, I am sure, to the toll that the final exams took on him, I managed to beat him although he is and has been a much better golfer than I ever was. He went on to win the RAF Golf Championship a few years later.

Finals passed, we began looking for work. I don't remember anyone then taking a year out before starting work – the need to make some money was paramount. The situation for us was very unlike that of the present day, where the new graduate destined for general practice is obliged or perhaps advised to spend three years in combined hospital/general practice roles in the guise of a trainee before he or she achieves final independence. In those days, once medical students had qualified, it was not obligatory to do house jobs in hospital, though it was considered advisable, and most people opted to do these house jobs soon after they qualified. However, since a houseman in those days in the Edinburgh Royal Infirmary got just his laundry and food and perhaps £50 per year, I had resolved to do an Assistantship first which would at least pay the princely sum of £300 per year along with my keep, before I returned to hospital life to do house jobs. In the event, the War supervened and any hospital experience I got was obtained in the Army.

After just a short break, and newly qualified, the next memorable phase in my life was the short assistantship I took up in the mining village of West Auckland in County Durham. I joined a family friend there, partly to be able to pay for the new suit which I had just acquired! Nowadays West Auckland is a model village, but at that time conditions there were like those encountered by Dr Manson in South Wales in A. J. Cronin's best seller, *The Citadel*. It had the makings of a pleasant village, with a wide main street, a village green, and just two big houses: one was the doctor's house where I lived, which boasted a tennis court, and a chauffeur for the Practice; the other belonged to the owner of the West Auckland Brewery whose product brightened my life there. The rest of the houses, however, were mainly back-to-back with outside toilets, a reflection of the poverty and underpaid status of the miners who worked hewing coal in seams just two feet high, exploited by their owners, and with men like Arthur Scargill to fight for them still many years in the future.

These County Durham miners, were short tough men who fought tuberculosis, which was then rife, and coal dust compounded with heavy smoking, but it was a privilege to work among them. They and their families were pure gold – the kindest people you could hope to meet – and they would give you what little they had; on my rounds in winter I was given many a welcome bowl of soup simply because I looked cold.

Conditions medically-speaking were primitive: I worked in the same (i.e. the only) consulting-room as my boss, which set privacy at a discount but helped in other ways, as I could watch all the time what he was doing. Ours was a dispensing practice, which meant we dispensed there and then as patients came in. There were measuring glasses for liquids, but I never found anything with which to weigh solids, and I used to watch the boss take a handful of say, potassium bromide, and toss it nonchalantly into a bottle. I would try to copy the amount when I had to do the same thing. On the nights when I wasn't delivering babies in squalor, I used to lie awake and wonder if I had poisoned anybody. They never seemed to take any hurt any more I suppose than the bottle did them any good.

I remember a bearded man who came in once a week all

the time I was there, saying, 'I'm no better', and getting a fresh bottle each time. By the end of my assistantship we were going round the shelves adding a touch of this and of that and particularly of tincture of asafoetida, which as its name implied was the most foul-tasting medicine ever inflicted upon man. It was quite true that he never got any better but at least he never seemed to get worse.

At that time in general practice there were many Assistants, sometimes as many as four to one Principal. They too, were often exploited, the Principal underpaying them, in spite of their doing the lion's share of the work. This was, of course, before the inauguration of the National Health Service, so in West Auckland a collector went round weekly from the Practice, collecting from each household sixpence (2½p in today's money) per head for each adult and child therein – not a vast sum, but even so many found it hard to keep up the payments.

I had originally intended to stay in West Auckland for a year, but circumstances changed dramatically. Having a few days' leave due, I made for St Andrews, as I did every year, and played in the Eden tournament there. I had no success in the golf, but I met a tall handsome Irish girl, on holiday like myself. During the short time available I spent evenings with her on the Kinkell Braes, a romantic spot above the East Sands, which is now, alas, a caravan park. More of this anon. Not long after we had parted, as I boarded the little train that used to chug its way all of four miles to join the express at Leuchars, an event took place which we had totally failed to foresee in the summer of our final year: war broke out.

I went up to Edinburgh one day, took the King's shilling and signed on for the RAMC. I remember doing this in an office of Scottish Command, which is now the Royal-Highland Hotel on the Bridges in Edinburgh. Coming out as

I went in was a student from my year, David Dick, who became a GP and anaesthetist in Strathpeffer, north of Inverness. In my turn, as I came out, I met a man in the year below me, Andy Ralley, who served in the same Division as myself and whom I eventually found already in practice in Carlisle when I came here post-war with the Doctors Willy and Alan Frazer. My Army number was 128375, so David was one number senior and Andy one number junior to me.

Whilst waiting to be called up, I did a locum in a practice in Stirlingshire. During my time there my employer, who had surgical inclinations, taught me how to take out tonsils in the consulting room. This was a bloody business, and it so happened around that time and afterwards, that one came across people with tonsils on one side of their throats only. The reason for this was that the unsuspecting victim had in the first instance submitted quite philosophically to the procedure but by the time one tonsil had been chopped out, there was no way he or she was going to part with the other!

CHAPTER THREE

Men will follow this Officer, if only out of sheer curiosity

On 20 April 1940 I reported to the RAMC Base Depot, Beckett's Park, Leeds, where I met up again with David Dick and Andy Ralley. It was the time of the 'phoney war' when both sides were cagey, largely building up their defences, so there was little action on the ground, though the war continued at sea and in the air. The Army reckoned that fourteen days was more than enough time to turn doctors into Officers and Gentlemen. We were drilled by a drill sergeant in the Warwicks whose complexion indicated a considerable number of battles, some of them in the Sergeants' Mess. Our uniforms hadn't arrived, so for the first week we were marched round the suburbs of Leeds looking scruffy and slovenly. The following week we looked equally slovenly, but by then at least we were in uniform. Someone watching us might well have got the idea there for *Dad's Army.*

At the end of this fortnight we scattered to our various postings; I, having requested a posting to a Highland formation found myself on the way to Perth to the HQ of the 9th Infantry Division, thence to be sent, still in 9th Division to Muir of Ord on the Black Isle north of Inverness, to the 175 Field Ambulance. Just to confuse the English, Black Isle is not an isle at all but a peninsula, and a rather fertile farmland one at that. Andy went somewhere else in the same Division but I didn't meet up with him again until we were in the South of England waiting to go abroad. David was posted to a Blood Transfusion Unit – where I don't know.

This was the time of Dunkirk, when the British Expeditionary Force in France, after a fighting retreat, was forced to evacuate under heavy fire at the port of that name and small boats of all descriptions swarmed across the Channel to help the Navy rescue the exhausted soldiers. Further along the French coast, on the beach at St Valéry, the 51st Highland Division, with which I served later, was not so lucky, being taken prisoner almost to a man from their GOC, General Fortune, down, most of them remaining incarcerated for the next five years.

Shortly after this the 9th Division became the 51st Highland, and we began to train, starting very much from scratch with ridiculously little equipment. At that time there was just one Brigade, in strength less than 5,000 men, and equipped largely with local commercial delivery trucks and the like, to guard the entire Highland coastline north of Inverness. We must really have looked like old Corporal Jones with his butcher's van in *Dad's Army*! Very slowly the void left by Dunkirk was filled.

Fortunately for us, life in the Highlands was peaceful in the extreme, food rationing nominal, and whisky abounding; in war time it was indeed a place for the fortunate and I was to have two years of it. During those two years I sampled life in a number of delightful small towns on the east side, like Strathpeffer, Nairn, and right up to John O'Groats where we trained in the colourful and wild surrounding countryside. Up in Caithness every second person is called McKay from the present Lord Chancellor downwards, and as half-Highlander I felt very much at home.

The RAMC is a non-combatant corps. Its officers wear pistols, in theory with which to defend their wounded. I used to practise with mine, but never hit much. Curiously and sadly, while in the Highlands I had to deal with the suicides – by revolver – of two of my friends, both in similar circumstances. Each had been carpeted and 'given a rocket' by their respective COs, and both had walked out to the woods and shot themselves through the head – two wasted lives! Regular Army discipline sometimes went over the score and COs could on occasion behave like Roman Emperors. Both the Padre and the MO had to try to keep their ears to the ground to anticipate trouble. In my experience, regular officers of senior rank came in two classes. They were either outstandingly clever, excellent psychologists and good at handling men, or they were like the Guards Officer in the story, who was so stupid that his fellow officers noticed it!

In that summer of these islands' greatest vulnerability, the code word 'Cromwell' was to be circulated to all the Armed Forces should the Germans actually land. It came through on 15 September 1940. We were at that time one company of a Field Ambulance billeted in the Portland Arms Hotel in Lybster, a pretty fishing village below Wick. Fortunately, a signal followed soon afterwards cancelling the message, these islands remained free, and we could get on with the party we had going. No-one would have cared too much that night if Hitler himself had parachuted into Lybster.

Shortly after this I was posted as Medical Officer to the 51st Divisional Reconnaissance Regiment, part of a newly-formed corps with a Battalion attached to each Infantry Division, the purpose of which was to scout in front of the divisional front in armoured cars and Bren carriers. I joined them in Drummuir Castle, Banffshire, a pleasant baroque edifice built by one of Nelson's captains named Duff, and financed no doubt with his share of the prize fund from Trafalgar.

Meanwhile on the romantic front, things were progressing nicely. Having contrived a couple more meetings with Hazel, the Irish girl I'd met in St Andrews, one in Belfast and one in Edinburgh, shortly afterwards I was granted leave to get married. As I mentioned in the previous chapter, Hazel is a Belfast girl, and the logistics of getting to that city from the Highlands in wartime for a wedding would have daunted a more faithful knight-errant, but we made it, I having got a flight there, and Hazel coming cross-country from Aldeburgh in Suffolk where she was teaching. The knot was tied on 4 June 1941, and I'm happy to say we are still together 59 years later. An only child, Hazel's Matron of Honour was her best friend, for whom Hazel had performed a similar duty four days earlier. My best man was my friend, the aforementioned Bill Russell, like myself a captain in the RAMC, whom the Army had obligingly stationed in Belfast at the time.

Since it was wartime, the Bride did not wear white, but an outfit of pleated skirt and short jacket in a greenish-yellow hue, which she thought would go well with my khaki. In the style of the day she wore over one eye a small hat; this, made by Hazel's mother from artificial flowers, was trimmed with two tails of velvet. The church was within walking distance of the house and we had a reception for 24 people with the last wedding cake made there, covered in white chocolate – a real luxury in wartime. Our three-day honeymoon at the Giant's Causeway was made possible by my father-in-law's closest friend, who lent us his car and gave us the petrol as a wedding present, petrol being otherwise unobtainable. Thence we returned by degrees to Drummuir accompanied by Hazel's Scottie, Andy, who was destined to be our constant companion until I embarked overseas.

Incidentally, in order to get from Inverness to Belfast at that time, it was necessary, unless one was flying, to take the train down into England and to wait on Carlisle Station for the Euston/Stranraer train which came in usually at some unearthly hour like 2 or 3 a.m. and which was invariably late. Having done this two or three times, I vowed to myself that I would never again set foot in that abominable place, Carlisle.... Little does one know what Fate has in store for one!

Drummuir Castle was an idyllic place for an extended honeymoon. Under peacetime conditions the Army MO is seldom overworked. While I was under canvas in the grounds of the Castle, Hazel was lodged in the stationmaster's cottage nearby, a rudimentary but very pleasant billet. The stationmaster's wife was pregnant at the time, and when my wife left three months or so later, the stationmaster's wife named her new baby Hazel. Baths were at a premium and my wife was granted the privilege of bathing at the Castle, which was all male. On each such occasion she was allocated a soldier to stand guard outside the bathroom – maybe with fixed bayonet, I don't remember!

The Colonel, a regular in the Argyll and Sutherland Highlanders was charged with the task of making an efficient fighting force in a short time from a series of detachments from the rest of the divisional regiments, and when a CO is ordered to contribute men, he doesn't send his best. Our CO, Lt-Col E.H. Grant was quite a hard man, a small man incidentally (so was Napoleon of course) but he had a difficult job to do and he did it well. His redeeming feature was his sense of humour. At the time when we were in Drummuir, the small fishing port of Buckie on the Moray Firth had the doubtful honour of the highest VD rate in the British Isles. Our Officers' Mess cook's footsteps strayed there one

Saturday night and he was on my sick parade a week later. I removed him from the cookhouse. Now, he was a very good cook, so the CO sent for me and there ensued the following dialogue:

'Did you remove Corporal Jones from our cookhouse, Doc?'

'Yes, sir.'

'Why?'

'Because he has gonorrhoea, sir.'

'Well, bloody put him back again. He doesn't put his Johnson in the soup does he?'

Incidentally, that same corporal had something I had never seen before and I imagine not too many other people have it either, before or since – that was an entire foxhunt tattooed down his back, hounds in full pursuit and the fox going to ground in the obvious place – a masterpiece!

We moved from Drummuir to Nairn, an attractive small town eighteen miles from Inverness on the Moray Firth which had a championship golf course. Here we spent six months in what was to be our last and longest stay in the Highlands. The citizens of Nairn showed the warmest hospitality to the 51st Highland Reconnaisance Regiment, which we never forgot. Hazel and I were billeted with Mr Morrison, the grocer, a good place to be during wartime rationing, and he and his wife spoilt us rotten with kindness. I played bridge weekly with the three local doctors who entertained me royally. Don't think it was entirely pleasure, however; we were away on schemes training for battle a few days at a time, crossing difficult country on some very stormy nights but I at least had as a rule a warmish truck to seek refuge in and tended to ride more than march.

One incident stays in my mind. We were parked in our trucks beside a wood. A ferret which was obviously fairly tame came through the woods towards us. One of the boys who had been a poacher in civil life jumped down, picked up the ferret, and promptly sold it for five shillings (25p) to a man coming down the road leading a horse. After that we didn't stay there more than another five minutes!

After two years this life of Riley was coming to an end. At the beginning of May 1942 we were ordered to mobilise, which meant moving to Aldershot and changing to a war footing preparatory to being sent overseas. The transfer to Aldershot entailed a journey by road, which took four days, armoured and tracked vehicles being slow-moving. I remember spending a night in Preston North End Football Ground on the way – definitely not the Ritz! Somewhere short of Oxford the column was stopped for half an hour. I and the Adjutant who was navigating, and in whose car I was riding, went into a nearby pub for a quick pint during the halt. A bit further on the Adjutant said, 'I'm a bit sleepy, George; take over.' I did. I followed the wrong river. In due course, in the blackout at 2 a.m. an armoured column three miles long landed in Basingstoke instead of Aldershot.... For some days I was less popular than Goebbels.

My faithful wife and her Scottie, Andy, joined me in Aldershot, and I was then sent to London for a Tropical Medicine course which gave us two weeks in the metropolis, made even more enjoyable by the fact that there was a complete lull in the bombing and nothing fell worse than rain. In the Army, if they sent you on something like a Tropical Medicine course you were more than likely to find yourself in due course in somewhere like Iceland. This time, however, we knew we were going abroad but had little idea where. I said goodbye to Hazel and Andy in our lodgings in Aldershot and we marched to the station and boarded a train for Gourock on the Clyde.

I have vivid memories of this particular journey, since at the many stops *en route*, the officers, myself included, turned out with revolvers drawn on the platform, to guard against desertions. As we steamed into Gourock, the Signals Sergeant, a man of excellent character and good record, went along to the toilet and put a bullet through his foot. With some difficulty, I got an ambulance and accompanied him to the Southern General Hospital in Glasgow only to be confronted on board on my return by a CO, furious at the slur on his Battalion, who said, 'Go and get him back – I want him on board this ship.' I went back, had difficulty in persuading the surgeon to release him, but eventually did return with the unfortunate sergeant, bullet now extracted, who was duly court-martialled and broken to Private on the voyage out. I had some sympathy with him, but he was a regular soldier and knew the score.

After the events at Gourock the voyage east in a large convoy was uneventful in comparison. As it so happened my luck during the War held right through nine sea voyages of varying length. We travelled on the *Stratheden*, which was the Commodore's ship of the P&O fleet, large and pretty comfortable; she carried the General and his staff with all the attendant spit and polish. One or two small details stay in my memory: the young soldiers suffered almost to a man from severe acne, not only on their faces but on their backs and fronts as well. By the time we reached Durban six weeks later however, the hot sun on their bare backs had brought about a complete cure – it was most dramatic to see. In the same connection I remember a young subaltern in the Black Watch who had one breast developed like a female. Whenever he walked shirtless across the deck he was followed wistfully by 3,000 pairs of eyes.

Our part of the convoy saw no enemy activity at all,

though as we passed Gibraltar, one troop ship which had been slightly damaged in enemy action had to be detached from the convoy and go into Gibraltar for repairs. Halfway down the coast of Africa, just past Freetown, a soldier of the Middlesex Regiment, a machine-gun battalion, was cleaning his weapon on board and put a bullet through his stomach. Though we had nine doctors on board, none of us could cope with this, and as happened only very rarely in wartime with ships in convoy, our vessel and its neighbour were stopped so that we could take aboard a surgical team. It is very unusual for ships at sea to be stopped in this way, and it was obviously felt that that part of the Atlantic Ocean was fairly certainly free of submarines. This event had a double benefit as the surgical team we imported not only coped with the patient, extracting the bullet so that he made a full recovery, but the surgeon also turned out to be a keen bridge player so we recruited him to our four which already included the future commander of the disastrous Airborne Landings at Arnhem who was known thereafter as General Urquhart of Arnhem; he was at that time a Lieutenant-Colonel and Chief Staff Officer of the Division.

Incidentally, I was to meet General Urquhart again some years later: one day after the end of the War I was driving with Hazel through the Stirlingshire town of Drymen and recalling that the general lived there we called 'on spec'. We found him mowing his lawn, but he welcomed us in for a drink and I mentioned to him John Rutherford, the friend with whom I had done my midwifery apprenticeship in Glasgow, and who had won an immediate MC with the Paras at Arnhem. The General remembered John well, having himself recommended him for the decoration, and highly praised his heroism. Dropped into the sea at the invasion of Sicily and then badly wounded at Arnhem, John was certainly a survivor, and I saw his obituary in the *Daily Telegraph* just a few weeks before writing this section.

After six weeks of over-feeding and under-exercising on board the *Stratheden*, we landed in Durban to the splendid singing voice of the White Lady who thus welcomed every troop-ship entering Durban throughout the entire war and to whom there is now a statue by the waterfront, something she richly deserved. Less pleasurable than the welcome in song was the discovery that I had to march seven miles to camp at Grayville Racecourse in the steamy heat of Durban. The MO normally expects to ride, not march at the back of the Regiment. I think that trip more nearly killed me than any subsequent dangers in the War.

We spent a week in Durban, and I believe we were destined for Singapore but, by the grace of God (for us) it fell while we were *en route* there, so we were diverted to Suez. Whilst we were back on the *Stratheden* at this particular time, Rommel was fighting the first battle of Alamein with General Auchinleck, and there was a 'flap' on in case Egypt and the Nile Delta should be lost. Consequently, all our senior officers from the Division were flown up to Cairo from Durban. This left just a Major as the senior officer on board, so the whole ship was much more 'laid back' and the voyage from Durban to Suez was pleasanter in consequence.

In the steamy heat of the Red Sea I was supposed to give an anaesthetic on board for a dentist trying to extract a tooth. The only anaesthetic available was open ether, and as fast as I poured it on it evaporated so the poor sufferer never went under. The dentist incidentally was Dr Taylor whom some of my Carlisle readers may remember in practice in Portland Square in Carlisle. I met up with him after the War one day when he slapped me on the back in the Midland Bank and reminded me of the incident.

After landing at Suez, we went by train to Ismailia on the Great Bitter Lake, part of the Canal, where I remember an ice-cream vendor shouting his wares on the platform: 'Lovely ice-cream, good for you, good for the stomach, good for damn all.' Thence we travelled to the Base Camp at Qassassin on the fringe of the desert. One problem here was that the nights were pitch dark, the desert featureless for the newcomer and the latrines were about 100 yards into the desert. Unless you had the foresight to take a back-bearing on a star, it was impossible to find the camp again, and many were left wandering in their pyjamas until dawn brought succour!

Similarly, I got lost. The regiment sent all its officers on a course on the sun compass, but forgot about me. Consequently, during the first exercise we did in the desert involving the whole regiment, my truck, the only one not tracked, stuck in the soft sand and the column went on over the horizon. By the time we had dug ourselves out having no idea what to do next or how to navigate by the sun, we had to wait for night when the Pole Star appeared, and by good luck rather than good judgement got back to base navigating by that.

Since Rommel was still threatening the Delta, we were moved quite soon to Cairo where we dug in on Gezira, the pleasure ground on an island in the Nile which had a club and polo grounds, a golf course, tennis courts and swimming pool, and where the Staff in Cairo disported themselves. Because of their always immaculate uniforms they were known as the Gabardine Swine.

We were at Gezira Island for about a fortnight. Unfortunately I didn't manage a game of golf for a number of reasons, the prime one being the fact that when you drove off a tee, a bird of prey was apt to swoop down and pinch your golf ball. In consequence of this, golf balls were very expensive on the black market and very few of us could afford them. Gezira was a meeting point for all sorts of old friends and I met a few of mine, in particular Jimmy Muir, a Highlander of similar age and stature to myself and a fellow medical student at Edinburgh University, who had been wounded in the lead-up to the first Battle of Alamein. Jimmy had been awarded an immediate DSO as a Lieutenant, something very rare indeed for a junior officer and an honour always regarded as likely to have qualified him for the Victoria Cross had he been further up the ranks. I knew that Jimmy had been wounded in a part of his anatomy most essential for the continuance of his line post-war. When I made enquiries about his recovery or otherwise, he assured me with enthusiasm that he had been able to carry out a trial run that very night and had no misgivings about the future.

Presently we were moved up behind the El Alamein line and then into the line itself where the Highland Division was sited on the right flank, with the Australian Ninth Division between us and the sea, and the New Zealanders inland again of us. I knew already that for some reason only one squadron of the Regiment to which I was Medical Officer was being sent in. I was a bit surprised when the CO sent for me and told me I was being sent with that squadron into action. It is more usual for the Battalion MO to have his Aid-Post with the Battalion HQ at the rear.

However, reconnaissance regiments were still then in the experimental stage, and for two or three weeks life was not too uncomfortable. We lived in bivouacs dug down into the desert where you could just get a camp bed but not much else, and ate in a Mess built of empty four-gallon petrol tins, of which there were any number around. There was very little shellfire, as both sides were consolidating there and didn't want to annoy the other too much. Sometimes we could get to the sea for a swim and would eat raw figs growing along the ocean shore. We didn't have too much to amuse us, but one thing that we learned, did. There was endemic in Egypt an illness called Bilharziasis, where a parasite got in through the feet and laid eggs with spines which got into the bladder causing much pain and blood loss. This could be contracted from bathing but more commonly in the Great Lakes on the Suez Canal than in the sea.

The Italians were in the line opposite us. We learned that the Italian Medical Director, General Castellani (who gave the medical world Castellani's paint for athlete's foot), believing, wrongly, that the Bilharzia parasite entered the body via the sexual organ, decreed that Italian bathing parties should wear condoms!

I had been in Cairo for only a day or two when 'Monty' arrived on the scene. Churchill had decided to replace Auchinleck and on the advice of his CIGS, Gen. Sir Alan Brooke, he appointed Lt-Gen. Sir Bernard Montgomery to command the Eighth Army in the Western Desert. Monty made his presence felt immediately! By his order all ranks from corpulent brigadiers downwards were on the Parade Grounds of Cairo at 7 a.m. every day doing PT. Monty never courted popularity throughout his career.

In Cairo, General Auchinleck, who had returned to command India, was reckoned to have had a raw deal. A little earlier, at the time when Rommel was threatening to break through, and the Eighth Army, commanded by General Neil Ritchie was in full retreat, Auchinleck had himself taken over command of the Eighth Army and had stopped Rommel at the battle of Alam Haifa, sometimes known as the first battle of Alamein. For this most crucial achievement History has given him little credit, although this, and not the subsequent battle of El Alamein, was most probably the turning point of the whole War. Churchill, who admired Auchinleck, said later that his dismissal was like shooting a magnificent stag!

Monty, as he was subsequently to do often, for example in Normandy in front of the fortress of Caen, waited until he had a considerable superiority of armour before launching the assault at El Alamein. In the event this proved wise, as a great many tanks were lost before the breakthrough was made eleven days later. Since the Battle of Alamein was largely a setpiece and many of the tanks were dug in hull down and used as artillery, the enemy Gunners could pick them off too easily and one could watch these melancholy happenings widespread, with appalling consequences for their crews.

I had only one close-up view of Monty, and that was at the end of the Desert Campaign, at the Triumphal Parade in Tripoli where he rode with Churchill in an open car, and I had a grandstand view of them both as my Medical Aid post was within touching distance. He was not universally popular, certainly not with his American Allies, and he was probably more popular with his Other Ranks – whom he believed in addressing and keeping in the picture – than with his Officers. Someone remarked of him that he was not a nice man – but then nice men don't win wars!

I have just remembered a story about Monty. This took place well after the War when he had become CIGS and was heading a party from the War Office carrying out an inspection of a newly-opened centre for examining potential officers. The party from the War Office were in civvies, as was the caretaker who received them. Monty asked him, 'Were you in the army, my man?'

'Yes, sir,' replied the caretaker, 'were you?' There was an appalled silence, broken eventually by Monty bursting out laughing and moving on.

The second battle of El Alamein began on 23 October 1942 at 10 o'clock at night with a barrage of 1000 guns, the biggest land barrage ever up to that date. I can testify to the noise, because I was positioned at that time very close to the 25-pounder field guns. When the barrage lifted, the flail tanks of the Royal Engineers (tanks with whirling flails at the front) beat their way through the minefield facing us and then marked with white tape the gaps made on either side. Through these gaps went the tanks of the 50th Royal Tank Regiment and our own carriers and armoured cars. I set up my own regimental Aid-Post at the far side of the gap in the main minefield, where ambulances could come forward eventually and operate as far forward as this gap. We were lucky to have Italian infantry facing us on the line, not German, as, while the Italian gunners had a high reputation, their Infantry was very much more suspect and many prisoners were taken here.

My apprenticeship was to be a short one. By dusk on the second evening of the battle we had been withdrawn behind the minefield, level again with the field guns, and as was quite common at dusk three German Stuka dive-bombers came over aiming for those guns and dropped a stick of bombs. I was standing talking to two of my colleagues. All three of us dived for a nearby slit trench. The first one in was OK, the second (myself) got a broken left humerus, and the third was killed. In due course I had a trip in the front of my own ambulance, to the CCS, about an hour's drive away over rough desert.

It so happened that the MO receiving casualties at the CCS was an old friend, in fact the son of the Professor Drennan mentioned in the previous chapter; he shot a dose of morphine into me and I knew no more until I had been operated on, the shrapnel removed and my arm set and plastered. I woke up on an ambulance train heading back to the Nile Delta, with a British Nursing Sister beside me asking if I would enjoy some 'M and V' (meat and veg), which I said I would – and did. That awakening was magical – it seemed as if one had one's own personal Valkyrie to bear one away from the battle. I remember walking down the train to talk to Corporal Cascarino whom I myself had evacuated just a few hours before, with an abdominal wound much more severe than my own injury. If he is still on this planet I would like to send him my regards here and now.

That ambulance train duly deposited us in the 106 South African Military Hospital in the Canal Zone again. I was doubly fortunate to be here, because it was decreed that all wounded of all nationalities held by this hospital would in due course be evacuated to South Africa to recover, and this duly happened.

One scene sticks in my mind. On the first night Sister Staffelberg, a buxom lass from Bulawayo came on duty in the officers' ward at 8 p.m. There were many changed faces in her ward and she liked to see for herself. She went round the beds whipping blankets back to reveal legs, or in my case a shoulder, in plaster. I saw my immediate neighbour, a major in the South African Gunners with a big handlebar moustache gripping hold of his blanket for dear life and, when it came to the tug of war with Sister, he won. I learned afterwards that for some reason he had just been circumcised.

Life was very good here for about three weeks. The South African girls were lively and the hospital much better supplied than our own, which tended to be slightly austere places where there was always more spit and polish. I don't remember ever having to sit at attention in the South African hospitals. Incidentally, while I remember, let me insert this concerning a British Military Hospital near the Dead Sea, where one day the following quatrain appeared on the notice-board in the Sister's sitting room:

As once Lot's wife looked back in horror
To watch God's vengeance blast Gomorrah,
So now the Sodom sunshine blisters
Queen Alexandra's Military Nursing Sisters.

– obviously written with feeling.

My next move was a short one, to the thirteenth British Military Hospital at Suez to await shipment to South Africa. Here we were a ward of convalescent walking wounded officers who used to go by bus in the mornings to the French Club in Port Tewfik where we spent the day. We returned in twos and threes to the ward where the day's ration of whisky, one per officer, would be laid out on a table. It wasn't too unusual for later arrivals to find empty glasses, and one or two officers passed out cold on their beds! Next we were moved to the hospital ship *Oranje*, pride of the Dutch Merchant Fleet, still on her maiden voyage, pristine and gleaming. Here we were fed like fighting cocks. Breakfast, as I remember it, included a fillet steak, bacon and egg and a full-sized pancake amongst other things. She was staffed in equal numbers by Australian and New Zealand nurses; tragically all the Australian nurses were drowned in a subsequent voyage, but not on *Oranje* which as far as I know is sailing the oceans still. Kipling has an epitaph on a nurse like those.

Ah, would swift ships had never been
  For then we ne'er had found
These harsh Aegean rocks between
  This little virgin drowned
Whom neither spouse nor child shall mourn
  But men she nursed through pain

And certain keels for whose return
The heathen look in vain.

The *Oranje* travelled very fast, all lights on, and Japanese submarines couldn't keep up. I shared a cabin with a Canadian Surgeon Lieutenant, and one morning we found on the door a notice: 'Jolly and Silverside – abortionists – bring your own hatpin'. I became friendly on board with a Flight Lieutenant Turner who, having won an MC in Malta for Air Sea Rescue in launches at the height of the bombardment, had been sent on leave to Cairo, where he had been hit on the head by a thug in the street and had fallen under a tram which took his left arm off. *His* luck hadn't held out.

There is one rider to my account of action at El Alamein, a rider which is both very personal and at the same time very public: you may recall that the Highland Division, which saw action at El Alamein had spent some time in the small town of Nairn. Fifty-four years after leaving Nairn, Hazel and I returned to the town on Sunday 25 May 1996, when a stained glass window, its costs underwritten by surviving members of the regiment and their families, was installed in Nairn Old Parish Church. The window itself, which I had the honour of unveiling, the work of Miss Eiledh Keith, a graduate of the Glasgow College of Art, is a colourful tribute to the men of the regiment. It incorporates the insignia of the Highland Division with the badge of the Reconnaissance Corps below it and below that the regimental tartan. Seventeen red stars scattered throughout represent the regimental dead at Alamein. The photograph (page 92) includes the Revd Iain Hamilton, minister of Nairn Old Parish Church, and Captain Leslie Meek. Captain Meek worked tirelessly to keep the Regimental Association alive and very active, constantly travelling the country to organise regimental reunions, maintaining written communication with one and all and ensuring that the regiment was represented at funerals, invariably being there himself to comfort the bereaved. This tireless effort is all the more laudable since Captain Meek was not even a regular officer but a Territorial, i.e. one who expends his own resources and strength on behalf of his fellows but is frequently overlooked when Honours are handed out.

CHAPTER FOUR

Sicily via South Africa and the Sudanese

After a very pleasant voyage from Suez we docked in Durban on New Year's Day, serenaded once again by the marvellous voice of the White Lady. We were then taken to Oribi Hospital just outside Pietermaritzburg, a delightful small town fifty miles north of Durban. Oribi Hospital had been created and expanded to accommodate most of the casualties of the Middle East and the Far East, and was very big indeed with many distinguished names on its staff. Here I met up with two of my colleagues, fellow casualties from my own regiment: Peter Bell, who owned Thirsk Racecourse, and Douglas Reith, my schoolmate and a nephew of Lord Reith who before the War had ruled the BBC with a rod of iron. Douglas, a regular, was killed later, a Brigade Major in the Korean War.

The time I spent at Oribi was an enjoyable four months. I was convalescing rapidly, and the townspeople were hospitality itself (this part of South Africa, Natal, is the most 'English' of all). The nursing staff were delightful, the hospital staffed fifty-fifty by South African girls and Canadian. Once the novelty had worn off, I got fed up with the enforced inactivity and with playing liar-dice and Poker, and volunteered to work. As a result, for a few weeks I was put in charge of the skin wards where by tradition your patients never die and they never get better.

Another ward in the hospital at Oribi housed alcoholic officers, evacuated apparently for that reason only; they would appear in the morning and go down to town and to the Club whose hospitality was extended to us all; here they spent the day and were brought back to hospital in the early evening much the worse for wear. It didn't strike us as an ideal treatment! In the First War they would probably have been shot. Perhaps the wheel has gone beyond full circle.

My father's older brother, Uncle Willy, who was by then deceased, had been Professor of Physiology in Cape Town, so I obtained a month's leave and went to stay with his widow, Aunt Aimée. The rail journey across the breadth of South Africa entailed two and a half days on the train and was fascinating. One travelled north through the Boer War towns of Kimberley and Ladysmith skirting the Drakensberg Mountains, then through the farmlands of the Orange Free State (getting off the train for a bath at Bloemfontein!), then across the bare Karoo to the wine-growing region of Paarl, finally crossing the fertile and spectacular Cape Province to Cape Town itself – fed on the train like fighting cocks again (the South Africans love their food and eat enormously being in no wise behind the Dutch – a lot of them are of Dutch ancestry anyway).

At this time my Aunt Aimée, who was half Afrikaner, was Red Cross Commissioner for Cape Town, and whilst staying with her I met a number of politicians including General Smuts in whose party I climbed Table Mountain. All the way up he was discoursing very learnedly on the botany of the mountain. Smuts was then regarded in our country as a staunch friend of Britain, which indeed he was, Churchill thinking very highly of him and seeking his advice on a great many occasions. However, in his own country he was esteemed more as a very astute politician; his nickname was 'Slim Janni' which means 'Cunning Johnny'. He remained a friend of Britain in spite of the fact that after the Boer War his wife had been held and treated none too well in one of our own Concentration Camps.

My stay with Aunt Aimée was enlivened not only by the excellent Cape wines (the Huguenots, my ancestors, having taken the recipes to the Cape) but also by my sixteen-year-old cousin's hobby, which was keeping snakes (some of them poisonous) in his bedroom. I was required to hold these creatures while he fed them with something that looked like an ear syringe – on balance, I think I felt more comfortable at Alamein! When this young man wanted more snakes he bought them by the yard at a snake-park and they arrived, believe it or not, by post. Another cousin, Gordon, had been invalided home from the Abyssinian Campaign with a nasty and persistent form of amoebic dysentery. He was a staff sergeant and I had the pleasure of his company constantly during the month I was there.

No city I have ever visited has left a more pleasant impression on my mind than Cape Town. Despite the spectacular rail journey I had taken to reach it, I had one small regret at having arrived by train, because to sail into Cape Town and see the city from the ocean with the backdrop of Table Mountain behind it must be stunning. A house and garden on the slopes of the mountain is the height of ambition for Cape Town's citizens. The downside, of course, is the proliferation of shanty towns such as unfortunately surround all the major South African cities. At that time too, apartheid was ever-present, and many times one witnessed black South Africans who were not supposed to walk on the pavement having forcibly pointed out the error of their ways by uniformed

Afrikaners. This often led to fights between these and our own soldiers passing through, who were only too keen to champion the cause of the underdog. Awareness of the apartheid system was uncomfortably heightened when we travelled in the transcontinental trains, very comfortably upholstered except for two coaches at the rear which were furnished with wooden seats and were often windowless – here the blacks were segregated. What a wonderful achievement of Nelson Mandela to outlaw apartheid! And it was surely no less creditable an achievement for President de Klerk, himself an Afrikaner, to have succeeded against a bitter faction of his own people.

Another memory of my time in Cape Town is of being shown round Groote Schuur, the hospital splendidly situated on the slopes of the mountain, where nearly thirty years later Christiaan Barnard was to perform the world's first heart transplant. There I was introduced to Professor Zimmerman who had succeeded my Uncle Willy as Professor of Physiology. In his laboratory he gave me a first-hand demonstration of the world's first test for pregnancy. It has gone down in England as the Hogben Test, taking its name from an English researcher, but Zimmerman maintained that he had been first and that it was his name it should have borne. The test itself was quite spectacular. A female frog was immersed overnight in the urine of the lady with the question mark. If the test was negative no change was visible the next morning, but if positive, the container would be dramatically flooded with tiny eggs from the oviduct of the frog and the lady in question would, as Swinburne alliteratively put it, shortly feel:

> her bosom-beats bound with the bliss-bringing bulk of a balm-breathing baby.

Before I left Cape Town I tested my rapidly-mending arm on the golf course and found it not wanting, so reckoned that I would fairly shortly be reporting for duty. The Springboks, with the exception of a minority of Germanic origin, and perhaps of the Dutch Reform Church whose creed was certainly not 'all men are equal', were hospitality itself to the temporary guests in their beautiful land. I well remember my Aunt taking me round her Afrikaner relations for Sunday lunch. We ate steadily from 1 o'clock to about 3 p.m. and then each guest was conducted to either a couch or a bed and was expected to sleep it off until 6 p.m. – a most admirable custom!

At this point I shall go off at a tangent to reflect on the songs of World War II. Each War has its song or songs, which the War itself tends to perpetuate by underlining the need of comfort for forces abroad and communities at home. The Boer War had *Dolly Gray*, the Great War, *Tipperary* and *Pack up your Troubles*. The Second World War had, in my view anyway, three, and curiously, none was English in origin. To my mind the number-one hit was *Lili Marlene*, the haunting and beautiful strains of which we heard for the first time before Alamein, wafting at night across the desert air to our own lines from behind the opposing German ones. Bit by bit we appropriated it and made it our own. It had been sung originally by Lale Andersen, a German singer for the Afrika Corps, and it wasn't long before it was translated into English and French and sung by Marlene Dietrich, among many others, but the German version was much the best and much the most evocative.

The second song – *Sarai Marais* – was taken up by our forces passing through South Africa and they were many, bound for the Middle and Far East. Originally written as an anti-British song, it must be remembered that, as I mentioned earlier in connection with General Smuts' wife, after the Boer War our own Administration committed many acts of cruelty in the concentration camps of South Africa. This left the Afrikaners very anti-British, a sentiment carried over into the last War in a strong and often very active extremist element akin to the contemporary IRA. Sarai Marais is also a love song and is often played as a military march and very stirring. During the past year in English Street, Carlisle, I heard the strains of distant music and walked along to the old Town Hall where I found the band of the Royal Marines playing. Presently they marched off, and swung round the corner into Fisher Street, smart as always, to the tune of *Sarai Marais* – and immediately my heart was back 52 years in Durban.

Tune number three is of Italian and French origin, the singer Cesarina Puccetti, who simplified her name to Rina Ketty, being the first to sing the French lyric to Dino Olivieri's beautiful melody, *Tomeri*. Not long after the first wave of transports on the Normandy coast had gone back for more, this lovely song *J'attendrai* was heard on more and more lips on the beachhead:

J'attendrai; le jour et la nuit j'attendrai ton retour....

My month's leave at an end, I boarded the train again at Cape Town most reluctantly, for I had loved the city and its people and had even managed a game of golf there, as I've said, without ill effect. Not too long after my return to Oribi Hospital I was medically boarded fit for active service and said my farewells to those I had come to know there. They included the man in the next bed who was a paraplegic and would never walk again. Fastened to his bedpost was his pet chameleon which turned blue on the blue bedcover, and on the white sheet was as white as the proverbial sheet.

I travelled down to Durban to await ship for the Middle East again. The ship turned out to be Polish, the *Jan Sobieski*, not too full and very comfortable. I shared a cabin with another casualty from Oribi Hospital, a Captain Porter, who had lost four toes off one foot and become known as the Pobble, after Lear's nonsense rhyme entitled *The Pobble Who Has No Toes*. The voyage back to Suez was once more uninterrupted and more like a pleasure cruise. I found my way to the RAMC depot at Alexandria, whence I tried to rejoin my own Highland Division, then in Tunisia. There were no vacancies there, so I accepted a posting to a Field Ambulance of the Sudan Defence Force which was then in Tripoli. This entailed another short and pleasant voyage through the Med.

Now rejoicing in the rank of *Bimbashi*, which had a romantic desert ring about it, I joined the Field Ambulance commanded by one Colonel Corkhill who believed so much in spit and polish that his Unit was known facetiously as Corkhill's Horse. At the time when I joined he was trying to make his officers do rifle drill; his officers, being doctors, had other ideas and were virtually on strike, since the Geneva Convention lays down that an Army doctor, whilst he may carry a revolver to defend his wounded, may not use any offensive weapon apart from that. Being in agreement I added myself to the opposition and as a result was posted as MO to a regiment of Nubians in the nearby desert.

They were jet-black chaps from the south of the Sudan, very fine physical specimens and I spent an enjoyable couple of months among them. They were really much more impressive than their white officers who were a pretty motley crowd, and whose attitude to their men was akin to that of the colonisers of the previous century. My morning sick parade was largely veterinary stuff for I spoke little Arabic, usually had no interpreter, and cases of things like leprosy kept popping up, which didn't feature too often in my usual working day. One was seldom overworked in the army (except in battle) and this was even more true for me here, owing partly to my Medical Orderly, Ombashi Salim who, if someone sustained a cut or a wound for instance, would stitch it up himself, inject morphine – and then send for me!

One afternoon each week I was entertained to tea by the Sudanese officers in their Mess. The officers did speak English and the conversation usually started with a discussion on English Literature (they were surprisingly well-read) and finished with their other priority – how to make their sexual powers stronger and longer-lasting. I don't believe they were badly served in this department in any case.

I found I always felt very well in the desert, which was pretty dry, and apart from desert sores, healthy. When I say dry, there was a sense in which it was dry for most other soldiers but not for us. At that time the allocation of beer was two bottles per head per week. An indent would go in weekly for about 1,000 bottles. The authorities never latched on to the fact that our soldiers were Muslims and consequently were not allowed to touch beer! Another item here in North Africa which I enjoyed greatly, being very fond of soup anywhere, was the groundnut soup which appeared most days on the menu, really delicious stuff that I have never come across anywhere else.

Whilst I was there the Regiment paraded for the Victory Celebrations in Tripoli and I had a close-up view of Churchill and Monty together; then the Regiment was ordered back to the Sudan. I went on board ship to see them off with another officer, called Alec, who was being left behind to clear up. We were in someone's cabin where the wine was flowing and we didn't hear the call – if there was one – of

'All ashore'. When we got on deck we were just leaving Tripoli harbour.... By the grace of God the pilot was still on board and we got off on his boat – otherwise we could not have disembarked before Alexandria, four days further on, to almost certain Court Martial: I began to think my lucky star was in the ascendant.

Rejoining 'Corkhill's Horse', I applied to him for a posting elsewhere, but since I was the only one of his Officers who played Chess and he and I played nightly under the palm trees, he refused to let me go and, moreover, confined me to camp for trying. A week or so later I learned on the grapevine that I was about to be posted to Kufra Oasis which lies about 800 miles south of Tripoli through virgin desert. Kufra did not appeal to me on several counts, the first and foremost being that I didn't think the transport that Corkhill's Horse possessed would ever reach Kufra, and that in consequence I would be eaten either by vultures or by the platoon of Nubians that I was due to take there. In any case, Kufra is and was a pioneering outpost and I am no pioneer – I like my creature comforts. I had heard that my medical boss in the Highland Division had recently been posted to Tripoli with the rank of Brigadier so he considerably outranked my present Lord and Master.... I therefore thumbed a lift into town and waited in Brigadier Galloway's office until he could see me. I described my present purgatory and said, 'Please sir, I want back to my old Division and yours, and I want to go to Sicily with them.' He replied, 'Son, you will be there tomorrow.' He was as good as his word: in two days I was on board the hospital ship *Devonshire* and back in the Highland Division in 174 Field Ambulance heading for Sicily.

We landed at Porto Paolo on the southern tip of Sicily. As D-Day landings go, it was a piece of cake. I had taken part in no preparations for this landing – indeed I landed with a toothbrush and not a lot more – so when I saw an open motor-launch reach the beach and without stopping run up the sand, I turned to my companion in astonishment. 'Oh yes,' he said, 'this is one of the new ducks' (amphibious vehicles known officially by their initials – DUKW – but pronounced duck). I was to be quite closely associated with these craft in Normandy a year or so later at the 'official' D-Day landings but at the time they were a revelation. The Sicily landing was almost unopposed and we now know there was a reason for this – Operation Mincemeat. This was cooked up (if you'll pardon the pun) by British intelligence, on the body of a British ex-soldier which was floated in enemy waters and recovered by the Germans. In short, the body was carrying documents to suggest to the Germans that the invasion would take place in Greece or Sardinia, not Sicily. This resulted in minimal opposition to the landings anywhere. Word had come back pre-landings, 'Mincemeat swallowed whole'.

Our first week in Sicily turned out to be a holiday in glorious weather. A ship carrying our Field Ambulance Transport had gone astray, so we had none for a whole week and couldn't catch up with the battle. All we could do in the daytime was swim and gorge ourselves on the tomatoes and grapes growing profusely everywhere outdoors. The only enemy activity was at night when planes came over to bomb the shipping. The biggest hazard we had was the bits of shrapnel that rained down from our own ack-ack, so we had to find something fairly sturdy to roof over our slit-trenches.

A week later we caught up with the battle, having liberated *en route* the Palace of Prince Borghese (and his wine cellar). For the next four months our Mess wine was served in very handsome crested decanters. If we ran out of wine anywhere there, our very splendid RC Padre, George Conlon, would step into the breach, going out into a village in the evening and saying, 'Io voglio poco vino per la Messa' – 'I'd like a little wine for Mass,' and the villagers would always see him (and us) supplied. He was a splendid character, George. He must have been well over 50 at that time but he liked the life and kept quiet about his age. I am not a Catholic but I always felt that the Catholic padres in the Army got much better onto the wavelength of the men in the ranks.

The campaign in Sicily was two-pronged: the Americans landed on the west side and fought their way up to Palermo; we landed on the east and fought our way up to Messina. In fact, the British attack was also two-pronged, with the eastern prong up the eastern coast where the countryside is flatter and the western prong in the mountainous country to the west of Mount Etna which itself is 12,000 feet high. My Field Ambulance was in the mountains, and we saw a spell of heavy fighting over, as I remember it, about a month. It was difficult for me to get to sleep here, since I usually found myself at the advanced dressing station where we were between the 25-pounder guns in front of us and the heavy mediums behind and firing over us. We learned to sleep sporadically when our own guns were firing, but if something from the other side landed near us, we woke up.

Here in the mountains the Germans were not the only enemy. Malaria was epidemic and malaria of the most severe and potentially fatal form we had ever encountered. Soldiers would be brought in with temperatures of up to 108° F. Since no one can sustain this temperature for more than a few minutes and live, treatment was most urgent. The victim was put on a stretcher, with a thermometer inserted in the rectum and was then covered in sheets which were continuously soaked in cold water from a hose. When the temperature was seen to have come down to about the 102°F mark, the cooling was stopped and the patient was warmed up and treated with liquids for shock – always an acute emergency!

Whilst passing through one of the mountain villages at this time, I remember stopping in my truck opposite a stall containing colourful aubergines and tomatoes. I asked a swarthy Sicilian sitting by his front door whether, if I bought some, his wife would cook them for me there and then. He answered 'yes' in broad American: it transpired he had served his apprenticeship as a gangster in America.... The vegetables tasted delicious, and we moved on in half an hour.

In due course we moved nearer to Messina, looking across the straits to the toe of Italy, and joined up with the other pincer-movement close to Messina. The Highland Division being earmarked for Normandy later on, we stayed in Sicily, and were later moved south to the village of Gesso not far from the lovely resort of Taormina. Here, not having much to do again, I set up a morning surgery in a cave for the Sicilians living there (all the local doctors had vanished) and did this for six weeks pretty busily, learning a little Italian in the process. My only reward was becoming known as 'il buon dottore'. Next we were moved to Augusta, a historic town to the south of Sicily. I have numerous memories of this time, all of them pleasant and amongst them that of the band of the Fifth Black Watch Regiment Beating the Retreat every evening in the town square. In my mind I can still see them marching off, the little bandy-legged drummer in the back row disappearing round the corner with his kilt swinging.

In Augusta I was assigned to look after the VD Clinic. One day, having business to do in the office of the Town Major (always a British Officer) I noticed that he had acquired a ravishingly beautiful Sicilian secretary. A couple of weeks later, I regret to say, he turned up in my Clinic.... After about four months in this paradise island with not too much to do, shipping became available to bring us home since we were destined for the Normandy landings. Our counterparts who had crossed the Straits of Messina were slowly and bitterly fighting their way up Italy – which reminds me of another 'Monty' story. In his memoirs he recalls a request he made from Italy in the winter of 1943:

> When the winter closed in on us, with the constant rain and appalling mud, I wrote to the War Office and asked the C.I.G.S. if he could send me out a waterproof suit, jacket and trousers of some mackintosh material. The Bishop of Southwark was to visit the Eighth Army to hold confirmations before Christmas, and he was given the suit to bring out to me. The following signal was sent me from the War Office when the suit had been handed over to the Bishop.
>
> We've despatched, *pour la guerre*,
> A mackintosh pair
> Of trousers and jacket, express;
> They are coming by air
> And are sent to you care
> Of the Bishop of Southwark, no less.
>
> So wherever you go
> From Pescara to Po,
> Through mud and morasses and ditches,
> You undoubtedly ought
> To be braced by the thought
> That the Church has laid hands on your breeches.
>
> We think they'll suffice
> (As they should at the price)
> To cover your flanks in the mêlée,
> And avert the malaise
> (In the Premier's phrase)
> Of a chill of the soft underbelly.

According to Moss,
(The outfitting Bros.)
'T won't matter, so stout is their fibre
If you happen to trip and go arse over tip
Like Horatius into the Tiber.

And you'll find – so we hope,
When you call on the Pope
That his blessing's more readily given
On learning the news
That your mackintosh trews
Were brought down by a Bishop from Heaven.[1]

The ship on which we were to travel home to prepare for the Normandy landings was the *Argentina*, an American ship, which held the 3,000 men of the Brigade I was in. All American ships were dry, which did not appeal too much to the Jocks. I had more luck because I assisted the *Argentina*'s MO, an American who gave me lunch and had a private stock of his own.

I also had a job on the ship's broadcasting staff (much later in my life I did two or three years as the Cumbrian radio doctor). On a Brains Trust broadcast on board, I remember arguing with the Brigadier, Nap Murray, that the Soviets would tone down after the War and become democratic and he said emphatically not. He was emphatically right! He went on later to become General Sir Horatio Murray and commanded the British Army of the Rhine.

The *Argentina* was travelling alone, so took a detour out into the Atlantic to avoid submarines, a tactic which proved successful though it meant the voyage was not a short one, but very pleasant nonetheless and once again free of alarms.

1 *Memoirs of Field Marshall Montgomery of Alamein*, (publisher's permissions sought).

We docked in Liverpool in late November 1943. I had been away for seventeen months, and when I telephoned home I found that my father was dying. I got leave straight away and managed to spend two days with him in Edinburgh before he died. My wife had been there during most of his final illness. Thence we travelled back to Gerrard's Cross in Buckinghamshire where my Unit was stationed. Here Hazel and I spent Christmas at *The Bull* and I managed to find lodgings for her afterwards in Gerrard's Cross at a house where the wife of the Persian Ambassador was also staying, to escape the London Blitz. They became friends.

After New Year I was posted to the King's Royal Rifles in King's Lynn, and told I would be there for three weeks. I duly reported to the KRR who had neither knowledge of nor use for me. I stayed in their Mess, where, since they were an upstage Regiment, the food and wine were excellent, and sent for my wife and Andy, her faithful Scottie. Having by now established a drill when it came to finding lodgings, Hazel went to enquire at the local Police Station on her arrival. Here she found a local schoolmaster who was a Special Constable and acting Inspector for the duration of War, and who, with his wife, very kindly housed them. These acts of kindness beyond the bounds of duty were very common in wartime and made up for the austerities. In addition this schoolmaster-turned-police-inspector had a close friend, a wealthy store-owner who had a billiard room and gave parties, and the old town of Kings Lynn itself was charming. After three weeks in Norfolk we returned to Gerrard's Cross refreshed, but still without the remotest idea why we had been to King's Lynn and ready, quite literally, for the battle to come.

At this time the invasion of Europe had become a certainty although it was perhaps not yet quite decided where; the decision may already have been taken but if so only the Planning Top Brass knew. The sudden preponderance of American GIs in uniforms much more dazzling than ours was a sure indication of a balloon about to go up. My posting to the village of Hedge End – then on the periphery of Southampton – left me in no doubt about where I was going to invade from. We knew before we went down to this area that we were to be attached to the 3rd Canadian Division for the landing and we therefore trained with them. Every possible subterfuge was being adopted at this time in an attempt to make the Germans believe the invasion was to take place in the Pas de Calais area, a good deal further east, and the bait was largely swallowed.

Training consisted chiefly of erecting and taking down tentage to make field hospitals both mobile and inconspicuous, as well as close to the sea for quick evacuation. Our accommodation consisted mainly of a reception area where casualties were received and classified, a resuscitation unit where acute casualties had urgent treatment for shock or burns, a Blood Transfusion Unit, and wards where casualties could remain overnight whilst awaiting evacuation the next day by sea.

In the event, after the invasion we spent only just over a fortnight in tents, after which we amalgamated with a similar unit to double our capacity and acquired premises, which had once been an approved school, at a small port called Vire. It was close to the beach for easy evacuation and we acquired twelve nursing sisters of the QAIMNS (Queen Alexandra's Imperial Military Nursing Sisters), becoming the only casualty evacuation point for the British 21 Army Group and the Canadian 3rd Army. But I'm getting ahead of myself. The invasion doesn't happen until the next chapter!

At this point I must include a story about the

aforementioned QAIMNS, or rather, about one of their number whom I will never forget. I have written about her elsewhere so I quote:

> I met her long ago when the world was in turmoil. I never even learned her name but I shall never forget her face. A junior officer in the Royal Army Medical Corps, I was standing in the corridor of the Cambridge Hospital in Aldershot not doing any particular harm to anyone when she came suddenly round the corner and I saw her for the first time. She was fully six feet tall, impressively proportioned and wore red tabs on her lapels, and the insignia of a Brigadier on her shoulder; she affected a hat of the male pattern which was encircled by a red band. She had with her a retinue of lesser luminaries of either sex fully half a dozen strong. I had never seen the like before in womanhood and never dreamed that such as she could exist. I did what any chivalrous young man would have done: I drew myself up to my full 5 foot 6 inches and gave her what passed with me for a smart salute. I also, making as it were a spot diagnosis – and this in fact is what proved to be my downfall – addressed myself to her, and said, 'Good morning, Matron.' She paused, the cavalcade with her, and returned my salute but with some lack of empathy I thought and she passed on.
>
> Halfway down the corridor she about turned and came back and addressed me. 'Young man,' she said, 'allow me to tell you something of our organisation. It just so happens I am not *a* Matron; I am *the* Principal Matron-in-Chief.' This said, she turned about and led her cohorts to the next engagement.
>
> Not long after this, Queen Alexandra's Imperial Military Nursing Service dropped the word Imperial from its title. I can rather imagine her voting against.

CHAPTER FIVE

Operation Overlord

I was posted as second-in-command to a Medical Unit which was to form part of a beach group for the invasion. A beach group consisted of one battalion of infantry, REs, RAMC and other specialist units, and landed early on D-Day with the function of remaining on the beach and organising it ready for the landings of the main assault groups, to pass through in due course. I duly reported to 8th Beach Group close to Southampton, where we were to spend a month or two in training. Here my marital bliss struck a snag as this was a forbidden area for wives and there was a search point on the trains at Winchester. However, once I had ascertained from the local District Nurse that she could put Hazel and Andy up, they both successfully passed the train check, concealed in the loo by enthusiastic other ranks, always eager to cock a snook at Authority. Some time later they did exactly the same thing, succeeding once again!

We trained in the Southampton area until June. Just before D-Day the assault force was inspected by King George VI. This event was a huge ceremonial parade. Since this was supposed to be war preparation of the utmost secrecy and the enemy was to be led to believe that it was to take place in the Pas de Calais area, I wondered at the time how such a parade near Southampton could ever be thought to be kept secret.

My own unit should have been led on by my commanding officer, who was at least a regular soldier, but he got 'flu and I had to do it. Fitting my lot correctly into the ceremonial park, in a parade bigger than Trooping the Colour, with my very limited knowledge of drill, was more terrifying than any battle I was ever in.

With the landing imminent, Hazel went back to Gerrard's Cross, and a day or two afterwards we boarded an LST (Landing Ship Tank) in company with countless other ships and embarked. We thought it was for real, but in fact it was just an exercise and we returned after a short cruise. I sent Hazel a phone message that Nurse was longing to see her! We embarked – and returned – a second time, but this time I managed to get up to London overnight and met my wife there. When we embarked a third time, we still didn't know if it was an exercise or not, but when the ship showed no signs of turning round this time, our questions were answered. The voyage across was not too rough for a flat-bottomed boat, part of this huge armada, unique in size and awesome to contemplate.

When the early June dawn broke and we first came on deck, the sight was like one I had never imagined – nor had anyone else: this vast armada, bigger even than that of King Xerxes of Persia who *counted them at break of day, and when the sun set, where were they?* This huge conjugation of ships was heading in the most orderly fashion and without opposition as yet, for the far coasts of Normandy. Had I known then what I now know, I might have been a good deal less fearful. The losses from the landing were ill-distributed. Of the five landing-beaches, two American, two British and one Canadian, the losses on four were surprisingly moderate. Only on Omaha Beach, with its frowning cliffs where the American Rangers landed, were the losses on an appalling scale, a scale which Tom Hanks' latest film does not minimise. Ironically, on subsequent visits to Normandy I have been in the Omaha Beach Golf Club, a post-war creation on the top of those very cliffs: *Plus ça change*...! A visit to the American cemetery close by, however, remains the most moving experience I know.

The Assault itself was scheduled to start at 8 a.m., called H Hour. We ourselves were supposed to land at H plus 4 hours, but were delayed for four hours in crossing, having gone slightly astray, and landed at H plus 8 hours, 4 o'clock in the afternoon. It was a very civilised landing – we didn't even get our feet wet. As we crossed the beach, the only enemy action we encountered was a single plane which flew so low over us that we watched it release one bomb and followed it down hypnotised as we hit the deck. It dropped into the soft sand and didn't explode, or I wouldn't be writing this. We moved onto the field adjacent to the beach and set up our tents. It was a tribute to the remarkable photographic reconnaissance for the landing that not only did we know in advance our field, but even which clump of bushes we were to be beside! We landed at a small resort, Bernières sur Mer, with the Third Canadian Division, in the British sector, on Gold Beach.

Looking back now across the years at the Normandy invasion, several elements remain outstandingly impressive: one was Pluto, the pipeline under the sea which supplied petrol; the second was the Mulberry Harbour, which, when reassembled, was to transform the pretty little resort of Arromanches into a deep-water port of high unloading capacity, invaluable to the invasion strategy, since the port of Cherbourg took some time to fall to the Americans. However, what impressed me most, then and now, was the overall super-efficiency of the planning. Every Beach functioned like a small trading estate, being largely self-sufficient, with a network of roads made of metallic substances unrolled from giant reels to unload tanks and for landing heavy vehicles. Each Beach was directed and controlled by a Beach-master belonging to that very versatile Corps, the Royal Engineers. However, all this miracle of organisation was still at the mercy of the weather of course, and the heavy storms which occurred unforeseen towards the middle of June very nearly scuppered the whole giant undertaking.

For a week or so on Gold Beach we remained within shell range, and were kept busy night and day. We had two surgical teams working with us, and I admired their courage in operating under fire, as the following story highlights. The Unit's dentist, Captain Hopkins, and I were playing bridge against the surgeon and his anaesthetist on a quiet afternoon in the third storey of the only house around still standing, when a number of bombers came over and dropped a stick of bombs close by. Hoppy and I were down the stairs and into the cellar before you could say knife. We returned sheepishly after five minutes to find surgeon and partner calmly arranging their cards – they hadn't moved.

My own personal responsibility during the first two or three weeks of the Invasion was Triage. This meant I had to examine each casualty and send him to the appropriate department, Surgery, Resuscitation, Transfusion or Evacuation, according to the individual needs.

We had in our stores an excellent concomitant of the Invasion at this location – the presence of tins of self-heating food. These were either soup, Horlicks or Ovaltine. Each tin had a fuse which could be lit from a cigarette and thirty seconds or so after the fuse had spluttered, you had piping hot food. One day we had a tent full of German SS POWs, walking wounded, and arrogant so-and-so's. They were noisy and objectionable. One of our RAMC Orderlies appeared suddenly at the door of the tent they were in and rolled in one of these tins, fuse lit and sputtering. Before you could say 'Heil Hitler' the occupants were crouching in the undergrowth all around. Another incident sticks in my mind. We had a German POW doctor and his four medical orderlies sleeping in adjacent slit trenches, when a lone bomber dropped a bomb at night which took the heads off the four orderlies and left the MO unscathed. He immediately got to work to attend the other casualties – a man to be admired!

Shortly after this we were moved, fused with a similar medical unit to make a unit of about 200 personnel, occupying a biggish set of buildings ten miles away but still very close to the beach. Here, along with three surgical teams, a blood transfusion unit and after another week, twelve nursing sisters of the QAIMNS, we became a hospital where all the casualties of the British sector came through. It was our job to hold them overnight and load them onto ships next morning. My own responsibility was loading the ships. These were either hospital ships, the two I recall by name being the *Duke of Rothesay* and the *Duke of Lancaster* (always referred to in signals, I remember, as the Dog of Roger and the Dog of Love) or the landing ship tanks (LSTs), of which there were many.

Landing ship tanks were used to bring over tanks in their tank decks, which were, like the car decks of a modern ferry, hollow. The side walls of these decks had racks to hold stretchers and could accommodate up to six hundred wounded. The LSTs were flat-bottomed, so when they came in they beached, dried out and opened their bows so that ambulances could drive straight aboard. If conditions were too rough for them to beach, casualties were loaded by DUKWs (which I mentioned in my account of the Sicily landing). These could carry eight stretchers lashed on and were able to swim right into the tank decks and be unloaded there. One could load an entire LST in about three hours, whereas a hospital ship took most of a day because the stretchers had to be loaded by tender. Each LST carried three doctors who did a bit of minor surgery on the way back.

It so happened that later in the landing I installed on a hospital ship a medical colleague from the same 8th Beach Group in the shape of Dr Hugh l'Etang who had been wounded. I bade him Godspeed for Albion and we didn't meet again for another 45 years, when he came to lecture to my Medical Society in his capacity as Editor of that prestigious journal, *The Practitioner.* He shook hands with me then immediately asked, 'George, what did you do with my pistol?' My mind traversed 45 years and I was able to remember that no one installed wounded on a hospital ship was permitted to keep his arms, and I had had a bit of coaxing to do with Hugh before he would part with his weapon.

Mine was a varied and agreeable job and very social too, as I got to know all the matrons of the hospital ships and the skippers of the LSTs, the latter of whom used to take such Normandy delicacies as Camembert across for me and post them in England to reach my wife in Edinburgh. The hospital ship matrons were sociable ladies and usually good for a gin in the late mornings. Tragically, one of these hospital ships was sunk and the Matron – who was a bit overweight – could not get through a porthole at a fateful moment and drowned. She had brightened the lives of so many wounded Britons.

At around 6 p.m. on one occasion when I was being entertained in the ward room of an LST, I was told that they were one doctor short. I telephoned ashore and managed to get a grudging consent from my HO there to my taking his place. Not being much of a surgeon, I gave the anaesthetics on the way over, arriving in Southampton around midnight. I hadn't very much time ashore as the LST was just boarding tanks, and then turning round for the return trip as soon as loading was complete. I attempted to ring my wife in Edinburgh from the house of a sympathetic butcher, to reassure her that I was as fit as a butcher's dog, but the lines were busy from that region and I failed to get through. I therefore delegated the task to the kindly butcher who got through in the small hours, and I got back quite safely without incident.

From where we were in Normandy it was only about a 20-minute drive to Bayeux, the first city to have been recaptured in the Invasion, and we would drive there in the evening for a couple of beers in the *Lion d'Or*, which I have visited often since. Whilst the battle had moved quite a long way west, inland from us, the city of Caen was still holding out despite being heavily and incessantly shelled by the 15 inch guns of *HMS Nelson* and *Renown* out to sea, which shells were almost as alarming when they passed over us as no doubt they were when they landed. We were constantly busy, of course, but life had its highlights. On Bastille Day, *Le Quatorze Juillet*, we had a party and danced, though perhaps it was ironic to be enjoying ourselves into the small hours when shells were still regularly passing overhead into Caen.

We stayed where we were, doing the job allotted to us, for a couple of months until casualty evacuation could be organised from the port of Cherbourg when that fell to the Americans. Then, when Caen finally fell to Montgomery's troops, we were ordered in there and set up in what little remained of the main hospital on top of the hill. The city was a shambles, its destruction approaching in appearance that of the German cities at the very end of the war. However, as most people will know, Caen's cathedral had miraculously survived practically unscathed from that heavy and continuous naval bombardment and a great many of the citizens had taken refuge there. We stayed for a week or two treating and evacuating residual casualties from the siege there, as well as those civilians who were left alive.

Then, as the Germans were on the retreat from France, we were ordered to move again and were a single Unit once more. We followed our own advancing troops until we reached Lille, where we stopped for the best part of a month occupying a chateau, *Mazurel*, where for the only time in my life before or since, I nightly descended two steps into my own black marble bath. Casting around for social life, Hoppy and I looked up the phone book and found the name MacDonald. This sounded promising so I rang up; although Mrs MacDonald turned out to be very French indeed and quite upstage she kindly invited the two of us to dinner. We dined in her very well-heeled house with a number of her friends who in due course invited us to theirs and Lille in general proved most hospitable. At the other end of the social spectrum, I was for three weeks in charge of the brothel area in Lille, and I learned one thing in particular, that, while they might look all right by night, they didn't look so hot in the cold light of day.

I left Lille with a number of new friends, most notably Dr Jean Carre, a gynaecologist and resistance hero, whose hospitality and that of his charming wife I had enjoyed and whom I returned to visit after the War was over. The Army, in its wisdom, posted us back to Caen once again after just three or four weeks in Lille – why, none of us ever knew. We went back and reoccupied the hospital on the top of the hill.

From Caen I succeeded in getting a short home leave and learned that my son Hugh was about to be born in Belfast. While waiting for the boat at the Transit Camp in Calais, I went into the cinema. The film *Mark Twain* was showing and, as I walked in, somebody was holding up a baby and saying, 'It's a boy.' I hadn't known before that what sex mine was, but I assumed (correctly) from then on that the baby was a boy. Hazel managed to produce Hugh on Burns' night, 25 January, a feat which sent her stock higher still in my Scots family. My mother used to send him a haggis on every birthday! Hazel and I managed a weekend leave in Dublin where I had to wear 'civvies' and found it extraordinary to see a town with its lights on at night as opposed to the ever-present blackout in the UK.

On arrival back in Caen, I was posted to Germany. However, at the time when my posting came through, I was involved in a Court Martial in Bayeux (not my own). It was a murder charge, and the trial took place in the precincts of the Cathedral at Bayeux. It held me back a week and I can't say I was heartbroken, because had I gone directly my posting came through, I would have been in time for the Rhine Crossing, which was perhaps the last of the more searching battles of the War. On the way up, at a Transit Camp right on the Maginot Line, I met glider pilots who had got away from Arnhem, and thus learned early on exactly what was happening there, as news of this disastrous operation hadn't yet broken.

Now *en route* to Germany, I joined the 52nd (Lowland) Division which, with typical Army flair, had trained as a Mountain Division and then been posted to one of the lowest points in Europe, Walcheren Island in Holland. Soon after their arrival there, I joined them and in a couple of days was posted out to replace Jack Comline, the MO of the 7th Cameronians, who had been wounded. Strangely enough, in another of those coincidences which seemed to occur throughout the war, I had been at school with him; he recovered and later became a surgeon in Rhodesia. I reached the

Battalion HQ in the evening as they dined formally in the open air off the regimental silver – beside a crossroad which was being intermittently shelled. The Army is unpredictable. I was back in action, which was to be quite as sharp as it was short-lived.

Over the next six weeks or so, we moved up through Germany sleeping nightly in a different village or town, usually moving into empty houses when the population had gone, quite often changing into clean underclothes which we found in drawers in the houses. Quite frequently too we would find a car stranded outside for lack of petrol and added it to our regimental column next morning, driving it ourselves. In due time there were as many civilian cars as army vehicles, and a sternly-worded order came down from Division that this practice would cease. We were on the last lap of our War now and approaching Bremen. After a couple of days' bombardment, the Cameronians fought their way into the city. Moving through the streets in a tailback of vehicles, I got out of my own truck and wandered into an adjacent large warehouse. Here, to my surprise and horror I found the dead from the previous day's bombing laid out in rows – housewives with handbags, shopping baskets and so on. If, on this last day of my War, I had needed anything to bring home to me the total futility and obscenity of it all, that was it. Neither side ever gains.

Now for a time we entered an unreal world. Hitler, when his empire was disintegrating, had laid it down that no German would stay inactive and that bands of what he called werewolves would not rest from sabotage when the Armistice was declared. Consequently, as we drove round the countryside through Divisions of German troops lying around still fully armed, we felt anything but comfortable. For a time, when driving at night, we felt sure that somebody somewhere would have stretched a wire across the road. Yet I never heard of any such anywhere at all. In due course we moved east to a pretty little town called Stendhal on the Elbe with the Russians just across the river.

Here I found myself in overall medical charge of a POW camp of all arms, including a number of German MOs. We were just one Battalion in charge of 10,000 troops and they could have destroyed us had they so chosen but no one was anything other than orderly and respectful. We stayed here several weeks and were then ordered to move back. When this imminent move became known to the German townspeople they were terrified – and with good reason, for the Russians were across the River Elbe and would straight away replace us in the town. We made the long journey in column across Germany to Belgium. On the way we passed the town of Celle, beside which Belsen had just been entered. I thank God that we weren't sent in there, as experiencing the horrors of that place at the start must have scarred the minds of everyone involved. We arrived at a village called Hautem St Leaven, near Alost. Once again I have no idea why we were sent here. We did nothing effective for a couple of weeks except to watch the main street of the village in fascination, because sometimes a tram would come through on the rails and sometimes a proper little steam train. One day the local GP took me into his surgery and I watched him successively take out the tonsils of five children from the ages of about eight to twelve. They were all put into another room to rest, and then paraded again in a couple of hours to see if the bleeding had stopped in their throats. Each child opened his or her mouth and showed the affected area, closed the mouth again and thanked the Doctor for his trouble in having operated on them. Recalling my pre-war experience of consulting-room tonsillectomies I thought to myself that Belgian children were both of stronger fibre and much more polite than ours.

Next we headed for the Ruhr and spent a month or so in a very industrialised part, not particularly attractive, but with one saving grace: it was summer and each of the villages or small towns had an excellent open-air swimming pool of which we took full advantage. Next came a move quite a long way south to a beautiful village called Altena in very luscious hill-country. Here the officers occupied a magnificent country house where the banqueting hall had both a wonderful chandelier and – above the mantelpiece and dominating the scene – a splendid portrait of a moustachioed German senior officer with a spiked helmet. One night when the CO was out, trouble started at dinner when someone threw an apple at this picture which went straight through the officer's forehead, through the canvas. Very soon the room was a shambles. I slunk cravenly off to bed. Although the Mess Staff cleared up very well, in the morning, when the CO came down to breakfast the chandelier had only two fronds instead of about a hundred. We were all carpeted by twos and given 'rockets'. I was told that as a qualified man I should have stopped it, but just as the Cameronian jocks were very hard to stop in war, trying to stop Cameronian officers in drink letting off the steam of a long war would have been like Canute trying to turn back the tide.

We moved thence to a village called Rahden, close to Minden and Lübecke which was to be my final resting-place, so to speak. Minden was where the British defeated the French in 1759 and Lübecke became the centre of the British Control Commission which was formed to administer a vanquished Germany, bringing swarms of civil servants in due course, mostly female. The Officers' Club there became our pleasure ground night after night. Our CO, Lieutenant-

Colonel W. J. Forbes was a tall youthful aristocratic-looking figure (a cousin of the Marquis of Aberdeen), who affected the kilt and a hound called Max which followed at his heels on parade. He looked good, and knew it, and was known to his Command as Bonny Prince Charlie.

In the village of Rahden a cupboardful of German signals fireworks turned up, and he took a notion to give a fireworks display for the village children. They congregated, all agog, in the village square, but as the first firework went up they ran under the nearest table or bed, small wonder no doubt – that was definitely a non-success. In a cupboard in our HQ I found a number-three iron, so we imported balls and laid out a course in the surrounding fields where we holed out in a stone cattle-trough, one in each field. This enterprise stood me in good stead, as the Director of Medical Services, British Army of the Rhine, who was a keen golfer, staged a tournament for his MOs at the Royal Club in Brussels. We emerged from all parts, myself after a seventeen-hour train journey in a packed troop train where I got precious little sleep and that little on the luggage rack. I got into the transit hotel in the Place du Nord in Brussels, had breakfast, asked how you got to the Royal Club, got onto a tram outside the hotel, paid my money, promptly fell asleep and woke up again back in the Place du Nord where I had started. I repeated the journey with more success, managed to win the scratch prize and still have an inscribed silver dish on my sideboard to prove it. I wouldn't like to tell you what my score was.

Life went on at Rahden through Christmas 1945 and New Year with an agreeable mixture of work and pleasure. I was really just marking time until my demob which came in January 1946. In fact, although I had never reckoned myself to be a soldierly man, I enjoyed my War and rated myself very lucky to have come in literally at the turn of the tide at

Alamein, and to have served all the time after that with advancing forces. It must be very different indeed when you are retreating, as was done so much by our forces in the early stages of the War, when the spectre of being taken prisoner was constantly on one's mind. I am duly grateful for my good fortune all through.

Once I left the umbrella of the Army, I didn't meet up with too many of my old Army friends. One exception I can think of is David Simpson, an Edinburgh lawyer and a Company Commander in the 7th Cameronians. In the still watches of the night when the wine had been flowing, he would enter my bedroom and insist on taking my temperature with a towel rail loosened from the wall. Later on in peacetime David became a member of the Royal & Ancient Golf Club, and in due course Secretary of its Rules of Golf Committee, which made him virtually the Arbiter of Golf Law around the world. I used to remind him of his dissolute past – and of Tennyson's lines:

> How many a father have I seen,
> A sober man among his boys
> Whose youth was full of foolish noise,
> Who wears his manhood hale and green.

In bringing these army reminiscences to a close, I'll include one or two items I recall which really happened and which appealed to me.

Not so long before the end of the campaign in the Western Desert, the Eighth Army captured a German paymaster endowed with sufficient money to pay the whole Afrika Corps. He was quite a senior officer, so Monty invited him to have dinner in his HQ Mess. The German had a glass or two and grew more and more complimentary about the treatment and respect he had received at the hands of the British other ranks who had captured him. He said he had asked for a written receipt for the money and this had been afforded him at once, without question. Monty asked for a sight of the document, which was passed over to him. It was unsigned and read as follows: 'This old bugger had a lot of money on him. Now he hasn't!'

This episode reminds me of a time later on, in an old Normandy beachhead, where I drove in a jeep to collect the pay for my Unit from the Paymaster of First Corps situated then in a tent at the village of Colombey-les-deux-Eglises, the burial place, if you are interested, of General de Gaulle. I got there to find a hole in the ground where the Paymaster's tent had been and my Unit got no pay that week.

Another story of another senior officer, very senior in years because he lived to be 100, General Sir Philip Christison who commanded a Corps in the Desert. During his retirement he was telling a friend that, when you became a grandfather, it was very important to live in a house with two bathrooms. The friend said, 'Yes, General, I see what you mean. I imagine if you suddenly sit on a celluloid duck it can be very uncomfortable.'

'Celluloid duck be damned', retorted the general. 'Have you ever sat on a soldier with fixed bayonet?'

CHAPTER SIX

Civvy Street and General Practice

We were demobbed by group numbers. Mine was 25 and that came due for demob on 26 January 1946. In another of those strange quirks of Fate, I was demobbed from Hadrian's Camp, Carlisle, a city I was destined to revisit. Although I had never considered myself a particularly soldierly man, I had enjoyed the Army and the picaresque existence which accompanied it in wartime, and I have to say that I missed the umbrella of the Army very much when I came out. The Army deals with all one's problems, and is literally mother and father. The hard necessity of making a living for wife and child loomed up and at that time, with the release of men from all arms, competition for jobs was intense.

Having first of all done a fortnight's refresher course in Edinburgh, I next did a couple of doctoring jobs, one in Liverpool and one in Lancashire which took up another fifteen months, and then came to Carlisle, thanks to my mother in Edinburgh whose close friend was a sister of the man I joined in Practice – Dr Matthew. Here I was also lucky, as I was made a partner in six months and became senior partner in another year and a half. At that time the Practice consisted of two partners and two assistants, and after my first six months there the National Health Service was brought in, and one partner, Dr Knight, had to decide which route to take, anaesthetist or general practitioner. He chose anaesthetist. Dr Matthew retired on grounds of age in another year. When I myself retired thirty-six years later, the practice had grown to eight partners.

The face of General Practice has changed beyond all recognition since then. In those days we had one receptionist, a seventeen-year-old called Nora Brown who was a tower of strength and who needed to be – she coped with the Panel Patients (mostly the breadwinners) who didn't pay, and their wives and offspring who did. This system in itself often created chaos. Nora coped like ten, calm and courteous but with an answer for everyone. I remember on one occasion the Practice Accountant asked her if she made any money elsewhere; she looked up demurely and replied, 'No, Mr Kyle, I have no immoral earnings!' Nora married Dr Ian Miller of Penrith, who gained a lovely and most accomplished wife.

In July 1948, as I mentioned earlier, the National Health Service came in like thunder, the brainchild of Aneurin Bevan, the Socialist Minister of Health, who had stood out for it to be a free service. This, while doubtless of benefit to the patients, nevertheless did us doctors a power of harm! Those earliest days of the NHS were a nightmare: we might not finish consulting until 9 p.m. after which often we had to do home visits. At that time, only a mother's first baby could be delivered in hospital, so we spent many nights out of bed delivering babies at home where we had often to do a forceps delivery and give the anaesthetic ourselves at the same time. Soldiering, even in battle, had been much less stressful!

Of course the National Health Service was ultimately a great boon to the country, but it was introduced far too precipitately without proper funds or forethought, and for the unfortunates who worked in all departments of it early on it was well-nigh calamitous. The fact that the service was free resulted in demands from patients for prescriptions for such things as cotton wool to stuff cushions, not to mention unnecessary night calls galore. I would have been the first to agree that there was a pressing need for a free Health Service – I only had to think back to my days as a medical student, working from a Dispensary in the slums of Edinburgh; there I had treated patients who, no matter how seriously ill they were, would probably live and die without seeing anyone with more medical knowledge than myself, simply because they had no money to pay for the additional medical expertise.

Gradually the NHS came out of the Dark Ages as far as GPs were concerned: in 1950 a High Court Judge, Lord Dankwerts, made an award that gave us a living wage without our having to take on an impossible number of patients. Quite soon afterwards the Government subsidised Receptionists to the tune of 70% of their salaries and quite soon after that Practice Nurses to the same degree. Gradually we became less and less of a cottage industry and there evolved the modern Group Practice with its team of Ancillaries which may easily now include chiropodists and counsellors. I was fortunate enough to be able to get an overview of these changes at first hand, because for many years I represented Carlisle at the London meetings of the British Medical Association where changes were negotiated with the Government and where we listened to many Health Ministers. The one who impressed me least was the late Enoch Powell who, I felt, had a brilliant mind, but lacked sensibility. The one I was most taken with was Harold Robinson, in Harold Wilson's Government, himself the son of a GP.

I have many pleasant memories of catching the sleeper from Carlisle to attend the BMA meetings, my sleeping compartment with a connecting door to that of my late friend, Dr

Harry Nelson, of Brampton, who represented Cumberland; we would share discussion and a half bottle of whisky on the way down. I never could sleep on sleepers, though they are somewhat smoother nowadays, and getting some rest *en route* to the meetings was always something of a problem. Sleeping tablets were not really an option, as they left one too doped for the meetings one had to attend sharpish the next morning. I remember the sad case of Dr J. S. Faulds, a distinguished Pathologist in Carlisle, who was going down to a London meeting of his Society: having taken two Secconal capsules before setting off for the midnight train, he was obliged to lie down on a flat barrow on the station platform and awoke just in time to see his train moving out.

The NHS was not the only arrival in 1948: that year saw the birth of our second child, a daughter, Celia. In due course she attended Miss Elton's Kindergarten. This was never an unqualified success, chiefly because Miss Elton and Celia had differing ideas on how a kindergarten should be run! However, Celia determined to demonstrate she could do it better herself by making a career of teaching that age group.

After Celia's arrival, my wife Hazel did not hesitate too long before digging herself into the fabric of Carlisle. She became Secretary of the Family Planning Clinic, which she ran for sixteen years. She was also on the original steering committee which introduced Age Concern into Carlisle. In addition she was organising secretary for Cancer Relief in the city, and secretary of the Abbeyfield which provided homes for the elderly. On a swing to the Tories she was elected to the Council in 1968 and came out again on a swing t'other way three years later. In addition to all these responsibilities she sustained, especially in the earlier years, the very busy and irregular life of the wife of an overworked General Practitioner, acting as receptionist and wife in alternating doses, and mother forbye.

Of our two children, Hugh, the elder, won a scholarship from his preparatory school to Fettes and there captained the school at cricket and hockey as well as being Head of House. Celia, not an intellectual, went to school at Cranley in Edinburgh where she acquired a Scots accent and won the character cup. She went on to Teacher Training College in Darlington where she was President of the Union. Hugh, following in his father's and grandfather's footsteps, studied Medicine in Edinburgh, and halfway through the course plighted his troth with the RAF who kindly paid his fees from then on, and a salary to boot, which bound him to the RAF for six years afterwards. This in turn enabled him to become a psychiatrist and he also emerged with an RAF Golf Championship, won in 1972. He is now in Sydney, whilst Celia became a Deputy Head in Newcastle.

As a family we are not exactly prolific: Hazel was an only child, I was one of two; we had just a son and daughter and my sister Wistaria, (whom I mentioned in the first chapter and who lived to be 84 and President of the National Council for Women for Scotland) also had two children, but not until she was approaching 40. Hugh has no children, Celia two, but they were not born until she was 37.

But back to 1948 – in those early post-war years petrol was still strictly rationed. As a GP I got a reasonable ration but had to demonstrate that I was using it responsibly. At that time there were no cars to be seen outside the Golf Clubhouse – the authorities would have pounced. So when I went to play golf, I turned into the village of Aglionby just opposite and into the first house, where dwelt Mr Pearce, the Carlisle Postmaster, a nice man and one of my patients, who not only housed my car but also revived me with whisky when I came back tired from my round.

As I look back now on almost a lifetime spent in General Practice, many patients stand out in my memory, most of them, curiously – or perhaps not – ladies. The first was in County Durham, where, you will recall, I did an Assistantship just before the outbreak of War. The lady in question was married to a coal miner (which one there wasn't?) and was a constant attender in the Surgery. I got fed up and referred her to a Consultant giving her, as was customary in those days, a letter for him into her own hand. On the way to her appointment with the great man she opened and read it. It contained the sentence, 'This lady is a born whiner.' A little later on, I had a very unpleasant session with her husband who had stationed himself between me and the door of their house (he was a small man, as I am, but much better muscled). It took all my powers of diplomacy – and I am generally reckoned to be a diplomat – to extricate myself from this. I learned a sharp lesson!

A little further on in my career, still pre-Carlisle, I was doing an evening surgery long before the luxury of the appointment system. There were still about ten people in the waiting room, and the outside door continued to open and shut ominously. It was a time when you either made a spot diagnosis and hoped for the best, or you took more than the accepted three minutes and the sufferers in the waiting room, belying the description 'patients', began to act like the mob in the Place de la Guillotine.

The lady who came in was thirtyish, not ill-favoured, with a teenage daughter at home, and she and I were not strangers. Sitting down she burst into tears, and my enquiries elicited the response, 'I'm two months pregnant. I haven't slept with my husband for six months. When he finds out, he'll kill me. I'm going into the river!' I could just hear the river not far from where I was sitting. I rapidly digested this information.

I had no reason to doubt any of it. Her husband had on more than one occasion been violent towards her and I had more than once suspected him of having designs on my own person.

This was long before the days of abortion on demand and in my area in particular there had to be compelling reasons – 'Who is the father?' I asked.

'Him up at number 35.' I had a mental picture of a smaller homologue of her husband! I thought quickly. 'Listen to me. You must stop crying and do your face up; it's three hours before *The White Ox* closes; get your husband there and when you go home tonight, woo him afresh. From what I know of him his knowledge of premature babies will be limited.'

And so it was done and double tragedy at least was averted. The baby was born in due time and if any suspicions were expressed they never reached me. Her mother and (supposed) father parted two or three years later, but without any further violence. When I look back on this incident, it is not with any great pride in my own part in it. But, as you may imagine, I followed the development of that particular child with more interest than usual. I was quite braced up years later when she came in to see me, a pretty nineteen-year-old, married and herself two months pregnant! What would you have done? What would the vicar have done?

Then there was Sandra, a very vivacious 25-year-old whose profession since the age of 19 had been that of fire-swallower, originally touring Britain, later most of Europe. When she came in to consult me, she would liven up my day with accounts of her amorous exploits far and wide. As far as I recall, I only once had to treat her for minor burns of the mouth.

Thinking of another patient now, I have to state with how

much dread I always viewed the arrival in my consulting room on a busy day of husband and wife together. Invariably, all the talking was done not by the one who ailed but by the spouse; most commonly the talking was done by the wife who had propelled her husband in, men of all ages from 16 years upwards – and perhaps most notably at that age – being by the far the less articulate sex. The difference at that age between the sexes was very marked; the boy, in those earlier days almost always acne-ridden, was gauche, repressed and fumbling for words: the girl, by contrast, was sharp and sure of herself. It doesn't in the least surprise me that the day has now come when so many top executives are women.

When husband and wife came together and the husband was the patient, the wife did the talking, giving a history concisely and effectively and quite often offering a diagnosis as well. If the husband were the spokesman for his wife, he would give a rambling story, quite often with a remarkable knowledge of intimate details about the regularity of her periods and even the amount of loss. Husbands accompanying their wives very often contrived to make it clear that they did not believe me competent to treat them. Some even managed to indicate to me that they wouldn't trust me very far alone with their wives.

I remember an incident early on, when I had occasion to examine behind my curtains a wife who had come in accompanied by her husband. I suddenly became aware that he had left his seat and was looking intently over my shoulder at what was going on. Then, adding insult to injury he took his pipe out of his pocket and lit it. In view of my experiences with husbands accompanying wives, I find myself in firm agreement with a statement I heard at University College Hospital by the well-known obstetrician, Mr J. D. S. Flew, who maintained that the proper place for a husband in the second stage of labour is the Public House!

Sometimes, as in the next two incidents, work and play join together to remind me of patients who have left rather smaller footprints on the sands of my memory. The first concerns Joe. Joe, an elderly bachelor, tended to consult me on social occasions (a tendency in which he was by no means alone). However, his best effort has to go down as the occasion when I was playing golf in a tie in the semi-final of the Club Championship. Joe was walking round. At the first hole I was getting an iron out of my bag to play my second to the first green, when I felt a hand between my shoulder blades and Joe said, 'You know, George, I've been getting a lot of pain here recently.'

Still on golf, the next was Fred. There was a new baby in Fred's family, and when the infant was four months old, I had Fred's wife consulting me in some distress, complaining that Fred was spending much too much time on the Golf Course. I said I would have a word and did so one day in the bar over a beer. I wasn't too optimistic about the outcome of our wee chat, so I was very gratified a week later when looking down from the Clubhouse I saw Fred at one end of the practice ground, the baby in a carrycot beside him. He hit his practice balls to the far end, then, picking up both bag and baby, trudged back to the other end and repeated the process. Some of the seeds at least had taken root.

Returning to the Clinical, I remember another man of about 50 in the days when tuberculosis was rife and a killer. Chest specialists largely did themselves out of a job by practically eliminating tuberculosis from the face of medicine. It now occurs only very sporadically. This unlucky patient of mine had contracted acute 'miliary' tuberculosis, which at that time was known colloquially as galloping consumption. When I first saw him he was to all intents and purposes dying

– bedridden, emaciated and with bedsores the size of soup plates. I started him straight away on injections of morphine to ease his passing. Extraordinarily, from the first injection he began to improve and presently rose from bed. The bedsores began to heal and within a couple of months he was able to go outside for little walks. By this time, however, he was addicted to morphine so I got him switched to Tincture of Opium which he drank in quantities every day like De Quincey, the Victorian author. To cut a long story short he lived for another three years and resumed one of his main roles in life as an ever-present supporter of Carlisle United. A long life in medicine has taught me never to give a firm prognosis.

The next two cases, both involving female patients, are similar in pattern. One night I was called out in the small hours by a daughter who said she thought her mother had died. The mother lived alone and when I reached the house I found it in darkness with the front door open – the daughter had been afraid to stay after life had left her mother and had gone to her own house nearby. I could find no light in the house so with some difficulty and the aid of my pencil torch found my way to a bedroom. When I shone the torch on the bed, sure enough there was a lifeless body, but, eerier still in that half-light, the head was totally hairless, the colour of white wax. This I have to admit I found rather unnerving until I realised that the deceased, whom I knew in life as having quite a luxuriant head of hair, had obviously worn a wig all the time I had been acquainted with her and I had never suspected anything.

A night call on another similar occasion brought me once more to a darkened house. I was an hour or so late in getting to this one since I had been at another call previously. Here again I could find no light nor sign of life in the house. I searched upstairs and found no one but when I opened the last door and shone my torch in, it lit up a ghostly white figure standing just ahead of me and looking at me. I had a strong inclination to turn and run from this newly-departed spirit, but when I collected myself and focused my torch again it became a tailor's dummy, also bald, observing me. The lady of the house hadn't been able to wait, so had phoned an ambulance and was already on her way to hospital by the time I arrived.

Another series of late calls which I remember well, since they were usually around midnight, was to a charming Catholic family whose grandmother had recurrent heart attacks with acute pain requiring morphine injections. Each time the call came for me or for one of my partners, the priest was called as well. If we arrived first, she had her injections, but if he did, she had the Last Rites first. Happily as I recall, she eventually recovered and the priest and I became very good friends in the process.

The next story I cannot claim as my own, though I rather wish I could. It comes from a colleague and friend of mine of a generation before – the late Dr J. B. Stevenson. A girl came into his Consulting Room distressed. 'What's the trouble?' he asked.

'It's the baby, Doctor.'

'What's wrong with the baby?'

'He won't feed.'

'Breast- or bottle-fed?'

'Breast.'

'Let me feel your breast,' said Dr Stevenson, leaning forward and slipping his hand under her bra. 'Just as I thought – next to no milk.' The girl was struggling for words and eventually they emerged.

'But Doctor – it's my sister's baby!'

Babies and pregnancies figure quite largely in the life of the average GP whether or not he takes an active role at the birth. In this connection two of the fair sex have kept a place in my mind. In the first incident, I received a call during my afternoon consulting hour: stomach pains. Two hours later, my surgery finished, I attended this call and was directed upstairs where I found a twenty-year-old girl in bed in great pain. On pulling back the bedclothes to examine her stomach I found a head in the process of being born; the rest of the baby – a full term baby – followed quite easily. Since nothing was ready in the house, I called an ambulance and passed mother and baby off onto a very unenthusiastic hospital.

Chatting to the grandmother afterwards I discovered that she had had no idea her granddaughter was pregnant nor had her granddaughters' two sisters, and – even more extraordinary – neither had the neighbours. It is hard to believe that this situation can exist in a family yet this was the second occasion I had come across it.

The previous occasion was when a patient came in to see me accompanied by her fourteen-year-old daughter. After consulting me herself she added as an afterthought that her daughter was overweight. When I weighed the girl she surely was, so as I was busy (when wasn't I?) I gave her a diet sheet and we parted. Ten days later I was called out to their house where the girl had had a fit. This seemed to be an eclamptic fit, as her blood pressure was raised and the hospital to which I sent her confirmed that this was a pregnancy over 28 weeks. It was terminated in hospital and the girl was none the worse. However, it taught me to keep my eyes a bit wider open, though I must say in mitigation that had it been the present day, I might have looked a bit more closely. At that time, though, such things were rarer in law-abiding Carlisle, and skirts were longer.

On a lighter 'baby' note, one more home visit stays in my mind. I was called out at 11 p.m. to a girl with a very new baby. It emerged that the reason for the call was that she had inadvertently put on the baby a nappy which had not been properly aired so was slightly damp and she wondered if it would do it any harm. In those days I still had a sense of humour and she was rather a pretty girl, so I forgave her, but I haven't forgotten her!

Still on the subject of the ladies, perhaps you will allow me to slip in a little story which my late friend, Bob Venters, ENT Surgeon, used to love to relate. In days gone by in Edinburgh the trams passed the Royal Infirmary. He was standing one day on the platform of a tram when a woman got on straight from the gynaecological outpatients. She had just had a rubber ring pessary (not used so much now) fitted to support a prolapse. It can't have been the right size, for it fell out onto the platform. A small boy standing beside the woman picked it up, held it aloft and announced in a loud voice, 'Hey, missus, you've dropped your bangle.'

Here's another true story with a gynaecological connection from my own Practice. In the days when cervical smears had very recently been introduced and were done only in hospital, I asked my receptionist to telephone the Infirmary and ask for information about when this test could be done. She rang up and said, 'I want to enquire about cervical smears.'

A voice at the other end said, 'Yes, certainly, which ward is he in?'

I had inherited from my predecessor in the Practice the office of Police Surgeon, a role which not only increased the number of night calls but also provided some lively scenes in the small hours. An account of one of these won a competition which I entered:

My Most Unforgettable Patient

Not many years after the last War, I was called out in my capacity as Police Surgeon in the small hours when my vital tide was not exactly at the full. I repaired to the best hotel in town where I found a slightly perplexed Detective Inspector, who told me there was a young lady in a bedroom on the first floor who maintained she had been violated whilst asleep by a man unknown. The DI was not disposed to lend too much credence to this story, and nor indeed was I.

We proceeded upstairs to Bedroom 15. There I was introduced to a young lady in bed in a fetching pink negligee. She was in something of a 'tizz' but to my mind it stopped short of acute distress – indeed, I thought her eyes had a reminiscent gleam. Nevertheless she stoutly maintained that she had gone to bed, gone to sleep and the next thing she had become aware of was a male figure opening the bedroom door in the gloom and afterwards stealing away.

Then, and then only she said, did she come to realise the fell purpose of her nocturnal visitor and raised the alarm. I banished the Inspector and questioned the lady in more detail. Her story rang true and I found it difficult to make her contradict herself. I followed up by examining her and the examination did nothing whatever to refute what she had said. I retired to consult with my police colleague.

Being a fairly new Police Surgeon, I had not emerged with any mementoes of the lady such as are dear to the Police, but the DI produced one or two hairs which he had found in the bed, and on account of these I was despatched back to obtain hairs from the lady's head and also from her pubic region. The former were unlikely to be relevant as she was a very bleached blonde, the latter quite possibly would be. The DI had previously elicited the fact that the lady's boyfriend, a company director (what a maligned section of the community they are) was also staying in the Hotel.

We considered the case afresh and finally reached the

The author's wife Hazel, and Andy, the two 'blockade breakers' (see page 64).

The officers of the 51st (Highlands) Reconnaissance Regiment at Aldershot on the eve of embarkation for the Middle East in 1942.

ateau Mazurel, in Lille, Northern France, where George was billeted in the autumn of 1944.

George in the park at Roubaix near Lille in the autumn of 1944.

Marston Lea, the house in

Carlisle Castle

George unveils the memorial to the 51st Reconnaissance Regiment at Nairn Parish Church. From the left, Captain Leslie Meek, Miss Eileidh Keith and the Reverend Iain Hamilton

conclusion that the whole story was a process of rationalisation to cover up possible eventualities as a result of naughtiness with the company director. I then left with a great desire for sleep – and a few misgivings. So much for Watson. Holmes lingered a little longer. He was on nights anyway and didn't have to get up in the morning. He paced up and down the corridor in question wrapped in thought, and as he reached the far end he became aware of loud snores from the occupant of a bedroom with a half-open door. Pushing the door a bit further open he found that the room contained a large man asleep in the bed, a chair with a top American Sergeant's uniform draped around it and a strong smell of bourbon. Not without difficulty he shook the occupant of the bed awake. 'Do you know anything about the young lady in Room 15 and the complaint she's made of an unwarranted assault on her privacy and person in bed?'

The Sergeant stretched himself – 'Sure', he said. 'The lady had her shoes outside the door and the key in the door. In my country that's an invitation. I didn't hesitate', he said. 'Neither did she!'

It was always a pleasure to work with the Police who treated us with every consideration they could. In earlier years the calls were often for alleged 'drunk in charge'. In those days, before the advent of blood tests and the like, one relied on making the accused walk the line, assessing their diction and co-ordination tests such as taking on and off their ties. Occasionally one met one's colleagues, which was embarrassing, and once I even had to examine my own Church Elder. I had no choice but to certify him unfit to drive. A true Christian, he bore me not the slightest ill-will and I have remained firm friends with him ever since. The accused had always the option of requesting his own doctor to be called out for a second opinion (if he would come) and I remember one memorable occasion, which still brings a smile to my face when I think of it, when the accused's own doctor was more drunk than the accused! Later on when blood tests were introduced for the alleged 'drunk in charge', our job was much easier as we simply had to leave our beds, take blood and go back again. There was (and is) no argument in Court against a blood test over the limit. The fee for this procedure was never particularly high at any time and on more than one occasion I would cheerfully have forfeited £100 rather than get out of my bed. When I finally came to retire, not having to get out of my bed was heaven. That, and having time to deal properly with a patient, a situation which the NHS has never allowed for, even in hospital practice where someone like a psychiatrist may only have half an hour to deal with a patient – not nearly long enough!

A night in the Police Station that stays in my memory was when the local police picked up two ex-soldiers from Glasgow, razor carriers, who had escaped from Carstairs, the Scottish Broadmoor. They had cut the throat of a male nurse on the way out, stolen a car, murdering again when stealing it, and had been picked up on what was then the Carlisle bypass. It was my job to examine them medically. Though they were small men, I didn't enjoy the experience, but at least the Police had stripped them mother-naked and there were four police to each man – two holding out their arms and two standing on their bare feet. They took no chances, for which I was very thankful.

Still on the darker side, I was called out to two separate hangings, both women, one of whom I had known slightly socially. There is something very particularly disturbing about entering a normal sitting room with a body still suspended in the air. The second woman, more distressing still, was a young married who had hanged herself on the back of her front door, opening directly onto the street. This was so that her husband would find her, as indeed he did when he put his key in the door in the early evening.

Before moving on from my experiences as a Police Surgeon, let me end on a lighter note – this was also a Police call but it was to one of my own patients, a schizophrenic and a rather nice man, as so many of them are, when not possessed. It was 1 a.m. and he had broken most of the windows in his council house. When I went upstairs to his bedroom he took one look at me and said to the accompanying Bobby, 'Get that bald-headed bloody vet out of my house.' I must confess that I found this comment a little bit hurtful, since though my hair has always been thin, I had kept it quite well and still do.

CHAPTER SEVEN

Hindsight and hospices

As I have already observed on several occasions, I realise how lucky I have been in many ways, not least to have lived and practised in the twentieth century, a century which saw the most astounding advances in the Science of Medicine taking place practically from the time when I enrolled as a medical student. One of these advances, which I shall outline for you shortly, had its origins in Carlisle, of all places.

I can also claim literally to have played a role, albeit only an observer's one, in this dawn of modern medicine. At the time I was a fourth-year medical student working in a surgical ward in Edinburgh Infirmary, and contracted a streptococcal infection of the thumb. This infection went right up my arm and the glands in my armpit swelled painfully. In those days this was dangerous, because if the glands didn't stop the infection, then the result was septicaemia, commonly known as blood poisoning, and was often fatal. It so happened that Edinburgh Infirmary had just obtained from Germany a small supply of a substance called Prontosil, for experimentation against the streptococcus. This substance had been researched by the drug firm Bayer which had already given the world aspirin.

My streptococcal infection receded with five injections of this potential wonder-drug, which was actually a derivative of the aniline dyes developed by the Germans. The drug was further developed in this country by the British firm of May & Baker and marketed under the name Sulfanilamide: it was effective against the streptococcus. Their second drug – Sulphapyridine – was successfully used against the pneuococcus, which caused pneumonia, its only slight drawback being a somewhat bizarre side-effect: it turned patients a rather alarming shade of blue, which tended – perhaps not surprisingly – to depress them exceedingly.

These drugs represented the first real, albeit partial, success against the streptococcus. This was the first hint of fulfilment of the dream of the Swiss bacteriologist, Ehrlich who won a Nobel Prize in 1908. His vision was of a panacea drug which he called Therapia Magna Sterilans – or, in simple English a complete cure-all. At that time the streptococcus was probably man's enemy number one, causing, among many other things, tonsillitis, rheumatic fever, puerperal sepsis (or childbed fever – another killer) and sometimes fatal complications of scarlet fever. Today scarlet fever is regarded as a rare and relatively mild illness, not a lot worse than a cold, but in days gone by its effects could be and often were, devastating. Just five generations ago, Archibald Campbell Tait, Dean of Carlisle, who lost five of his daughters in the scarlet fever epidemic of 1856, wrote thus in the front of his Prayer Book – a poignant record of what families had to face in the days before the advent of antibiotics:

> I used this book at the funerals of my dearest children Charlotte and Susan on 10th and 12th of March 1856. Also – alas! – of my sweet Frances on Good Friday the 21st and of my eldest born, my darling, sainted Catty on Wednesday after Easter, the 26th, the day after the anniversary of her baptism.
>
> Also – woe's me – how shall I write it – of my bright Mary on the 10th of April.

The M & B drugs were bacterio-static, that is they checked the activities of the streptococci without actually killing them. The next phase, which came a year or two later was the development of antibiotics, penicillin being first in the field; these were bactericidal meaning they killed the germ. These were about to enter the arena, spearheaded by a mould like that on cheese, observed by Alexander Fleming to inhibit the growth of germs on a culture plate.

Penicillin was and still is the wonder drug. I first met it in the Western Desert. In those days we gave very small doses by injection, which hurt like fury. Penicillin changed the face of medicine overnight, virtually eliminating syphilis, which had been the biggest scourge in society from Henry VIII downwards. (Syphilis, however, was not the reason for the madness, now immortalised on film, of that other famous monarch, George III. His madness was caused by another illness, porphyria.) Penicillin also cured gonorrhoea with just one injection so that the venereology clinics in every hospital gradually ceased to be.

Parallel antibiotics like Streptomycin were also developed to cure tuberculosis, which at the time was probably our biggest killer. (The poet John Keats, himself a medical student, died of it in Rome aged 26.) When I qualified some vaccines were already in use for diseases such as typhoid, cholera and diphtheria and were effective, little by little, in eliminating these illnesses in this country. Diphtheria was especially distressing, because sometimes the membrane closed the victim's throat and the only way to save the patient's life was by performing a tracheotomy. Another disease that I saw practically eliminated by prophylactic vaccination in my time, was poliomyelitis; there can be few illnesses more distressing for a mother of young children to witness, and in my early days in general practice I saw many young people with paralysis resulting from a bout of poliomyelitis.

The advent of such antibiotics was undoubtedly the most significant advance ever in the field of Medicine, but there was also another, quite comparable, but possibly less appreciated in significance nowadays, the effects of which were almost as dramatic in the saving of lives. This breakthrough involved not only my native city, Edinburgh, but, less likely perhaps, my adopted city of Carlisle.

Joseph Lister (1827–1921) was born in London and graduated from University College. He went to Edinburgh in 1853 to work as Assistant to the Professor of Surgery there, the celebrated James Syme, occasionally performing surgery in the Edinburgh Royal Infirmary. In the following year he was appointed Lecturer in Surgery. At the time Lister was visiting a slaughterhouse to conduct experiments in blood coagulation.

In 1856 Lister married Syme's daughter and was appointed Regius Professor of Surgery in Glasgow. Nine years later he was studying the work of Pasteur in the breeding of microbes in dirt, and shortly afterwards heard that carbolic acid was being used for the purification of sewage in Carlisle. Putting together these ideas he heralded the wonderful era of antisepsis in surgery and most other aspects of medicine. Lister moved back to Edinburgh to the Chair of Surgery and thence to be Professor in London. By that time antisepsis was the norm worldwide.

Becoming a Baronet in 1883 he retired 10 years later. In 1898 he was presented with the Freedom of the city of Edinburgh. He was the first Doctor to be made President of the Royal Society and the first to receive a Peerage.

The advent of antibiotics and of antisepsis undoubtedly changed the face of Medicine in the last century, but there have been other, different, but equally important changes in other areas. One of these significant developments is the rise of the Hospice for the care of the terminally ill. Were I to be suffering from an incurable disease and not able to spend my last days in my own home, I would hope to be fortunate enough to spend them in a Hospice. I became personally interested in the Hospice movement a decade or so ago, because my niece, Jane, was Sister-in-Charge of one of the earlier ones, St. Columba's, on the shores of the Firth of Forth in Edinburgh. I paid several visits to this hospice, and my sister died there a few years ago, so I welcomed the advent of the Eden Valley Hospice here in Carlisle.

The Eden Valley Hospice opened in 1993 and created and maintained by voluntary contribution, is the fruit of long and continuing work on the part of very many dedicated people. I think we all have the feeling, 'There but for the grace of God, go I.' Eden Valley has been designed with imagination and understanding, and its staff are gifted and dedicated people, the reason being that they are dealing day and night with this single problem of mortality and become completely expert in handling it.

Not only the patients but their families as well receive every help and consideration. Of course, even in a hospice, as anywhere else, morphine and heroin are addictive drugs, but in the hospice they achieve a near-miraculous effect, rather than the destructive effect created for example in the world of drug-addiction. In my own lifetime I have only ever twice received an injection of morphine, on the first occasion by my own hand: I was in the Army under canvas in November, on a bleak moor in Caithness, with rain pouring down and with acute toothache. By 1 a.m. I could stand it no longer so I got up and gave myself a quarter of a grain of morphine by injection. The effect was magical. The second occasion was in the CCS at Alamein. The effect again was instant and magical! The qualities of these drugs being what they are, I feel that if they are indicated, they should be used as early as possible once a diagnosis of incurable cancer is confirmed and pain is mounting. Out in the field in General Practice, if the patient is being nursed at home, the GP, knowing both patient and family, can judge the moment when distress should give way to artificially-induced euphoria. In a Hospice the Staff are trained and sensitive equally to judge that moment, from which most usually there is no turning back, once strong drugs have been used.

There still exists in this country some conflict between the American practice of spelling out to the patient early on that he has cancer and will probably die of it, and the more traditional approach here which is to talk round the subject as long as possible. Personally, I have always believed that no one should ever be deprived of hope, as miracles are not unknown in Medicine. I think there is an absolute obligation on the part of the Doctor to tell the next of kin the exact situation, and indeed this is generally accepted. Likewise, if the patient asks point blank, 'Have I got cancer?', or 'Am I going to die?' he or she must be given a straight answer. Few patients do ask, however, and more often than not they can be soothed into a state of comparative limbo with narcotic drugs and the question isn't asked at all.

In my experience, I found that often a patient who was getting a bit far through was already a little sedated and his sharpness of thought was correspondingly somewhat blunted, even if he had not by that time been moved onto the terminal drugs like morphine or heroin. Sometimes such a patient would ask his wife and since she knew the facts, she could use her own discretion as to how or if she would tell him. I always believed that patients, especially those still in the prime of life with perhaps even a young family, did not necessarily want to have the cold blunt truth spelled out. However, if I were quite sure in my own mind that a patient was nearing the terminal stage I would not hesitate to start the terminal drugs in doses strong enough to create a quick euphoria. One reason why Hospices are so successful in caring for the terminally ill is that they don't hold back from using such drugs at a relatively early stage.

Sometimes, but not too often, religious beliefs – either those of the patient or of the spouse – come into the equation and dictate a different approach. My own outlook in practice has been, 'If possible I must not do away with Hope!' but sometimes down the years I have suspected myself of moral cowardice!

Another major change that I have witnessed on the medico-social scene – and one that I am not unequivocally enthusiastic about – is the introduction, and, one might even say, the galloping spread, of counselling. Forty to fifty years ago any counselling – and it wasn't much – was done by the family doctor when he had time. Nowadays, since it appears that there is even less time available, counsellors have spring up all round the countryside like toadstools. No doubt they meet a need, most especially for people who want to unburden themselves at length to a sympathetic listener – a facility never over-available anywhere before in an overworked Health Service. Some Practices now employ a lay counsellor to complement the work of the doctors.

Unfortunately, nowadays 'counselling' tends to come hand in hand with her ugly sister, 'compensation', a state of affairs which is already creating and will continue to create an increasing problem in this generation. Imagine the reaction and comments of a man or woman who had worked solidly through the Blitz in Liverpool, Glasgow or Belfast, or of a Surgeon who operated steadily through the Blitz in East

London, on learning that some policemen on Merseyside were to be compensated for what they saw in one afternoon at Hillsborough. All the money in Fort Knox wouldn't have compensated the British Army on the Somme in World War I. In an age where Religion is declining, the god of Mammon seems to be holding his own pretty well.

When the American Forces came over to England in the last War they were issued with leaflets which said, 'Don't be deceived and think that the British are a bit prissy. The English language wasn't spread right round the world by a race of panty-waists!' The compensation obsession, so rapidly spreading throughout America is recognised as an unfortunate regression to the infant mentality – and one which appears to be catching on here too.

It is the spread of this compensation mentality to this country which, tragically, makes the members of the medical profession within the NHS, of whatever branch, want to get out and draw their pensions at the earliest possible moment with premature loss of trained medical talent. Most certainly, collectively now the medical profession feels somebody constantly looking over its shoulder. A compensation suit, even though it may be ultimately settled by insurance, brings anguish, stress and loss of prestige far out of proportion to the incident which triggered it. We didn't know the meaning of the term here in Britain until 50 years or so ago when American Interns began chasing ambulances!

This short sketch about counselling, written 25 years ago by me still seems to have some relevance:

Conduct Unbecoming

She came in last Wednesday, latish on in the morning surgery, a comely woman, I know her well, around two score and ten, with a complexion which would do credit to either of her daughters-in-law who think the world of her. She made herself comfortable. 'How are you?' she said. 'We never ask how the doctor is.'

As a matter of fact she does, always has – and normally I turn the question with a light laugh by saying, 'I'm alive', or 'Holding together', or 'Still getting round the Golf Course in the late eighties'. I don't know what came over me that morning. 'For some weeks,' I found myself saying, 'I've been getting not exactly a pain, but discomfort in my tummy which starts on the right and works round to the left and, as you can see, I am distended. I'm tired, yet I don't sleep and I find it hard to talk to people except perhaps you, and I'm not getting enjoyment out of a long surgery like I used to and feel I should. I find myself crying for no reason. I can be cleaning the car and I find myself in tears.'

At this point I began to cry. She moved her chair a little and before I knew where I was, a plump arm was round my shoulder and my senses were imbued with relief and Chanel No. 5, both pleasurable.

'I can't', I sobbed, 'talk to my wife any more. She puts the children first and doesn't seem to want to listen. Besides this, she has taken to staying out in the evening; she didn't come in till 11 p.m. on Friday and that isn't her WRVS night. I can't help wondering, especially since I've put on all this weight why lady patients, always excepting yourself, don't seem to want to spend so much time consulting me nowadays. Sometimes I'm home by 6.30 p.m. I feel so ashamed; I'm going through half a bottle of Bell's a day now, whereas six months ago it was one Tio Pepe before dinner.'

She withdrew her arm gently and contemplated me as I composed myself, her soft brown eyes alight with understanding and compassion. 'I would like', she said, 'to see you again on Thursday. I shall make another appointment.'

I watched her ample back all the way to the door and I felt, in keeping perhaps with my recent behaviour, if you will excuse the simile, like an engorged breast to which the baby has been put, but which it has reneged on after just five minutes. Or to change the simile, like an iceberg – there was so much more below the surface!

I pressed the buzzer and sat back in my chair, half-expectant. Perhaps fortunately for my standing in the Practice, the next patient turned out to be one of our hardworking core of dustmen, still in his working clothes!

CHAPTER EIGHT

Hypnosis and Hypnotherapy

In my early fifties, as you will read in a subsequent chapter, I had a Coronary, and afterwards began looking for a way of life that didn't involve jumping hurriedly out of bed several times a week – a practice which had lost its charm once I was past the age of 50. In 1969, I took to practising hypnotherapy. Having always been more interested in the mind than the body, I had read a little about the use of hypnosis in medicine. At that time hypnosis was just beginning to be used universally, and perhaps more importantly, had begun to be accepted as respectable and was slowly losing its longstanding aura of witchcraft amongst people in general.

The power of hypnosis has been recognised from the earliest times but probably gained its effects mostly from fear. The ancient Greek temples like the Temple of Diana at Ephesus contained an oracle, a disembodied voice which proclaimed in awesome tones to a rapt audience what was to happen in the future; this they believed implicitly and so made it happen. It seems likely that Christ in His teaching had a stronger hypnotic influence and presence than anyone before or since.

In the Middle Ages hypnotism went underground rather, as the Church wanted to have a monopoly on miracles, and if you indulged in them you might be burnt at the stake as were the Witches of Salem in the early days of American colonisation.

Hypnosis linked with some kind of medical treatment did not surface until the mid-eighteenth century, when an Austrian named Franz Anton Mesmer began to practise in Paris. Mesmer gave a new word to the language, mesmerism: we have all been 'mesmerised' like a rabbit in the headlamps of a car. Mesmer set up mass treatment in Paris and soon had a flourishing practice among the well-to-do. He brought about cures in conditions where no one had had success before. It was his custom to have patients sitting in a circle in groups, round a wooden tub containing iron filings and sulphuric acid and with iron rods protruding from it, which those assembled grasped.

Mesmer presided over the assembled company, and wearing something akin to a hat, made suggestions – he suggested that what he called animal magnetism would pass from the tub into their bodies and would bring about a cure for whatever they suffered from. He got cures, and his reputation spread in consequence, but the cures were due not to the iron filings, which were irrelevant, but to the positive suggestions he gave to people who had no positive alternative at that time since orthodox medicine was so appalling and offered no hope of a cure for anything. Mesmer was a showman, the Paul McKenna of his time, with soft music playing to heighten the effect of what he was suggesting.

In due time the medical establishment, partly envious, took action and a Tribunal was set up to examine the bona fides of Franz Mesmer. This tribunal included the famous American scientist, Benjamin Franklin as well as Dr Guillotine, inventor of the eponymous machine of death who, incidentally, in due course suffered the same fate as Deacon Brodie in Edinburgh, who also invented a machine of death on which he eventually perished himself. The Tribunal concluded that Mesmer was a charlatan and he disappeared from prominence, but disciples of Mesmer kept his practices going, and these disciples became known as magnetisers. One of them is said many years later to have treated Mary Baker Eddy in America for a spinal injury; she in due course attributed her recovery to divine intervention and duly founded the mighty and wealthy Christian Science Church.

This form of treatment was re-christened Hypnosis by a Manchester dental surgeon in 1842; the term derives from the Greek word *hypnos* – sleep, although it is not, in fact, a state of sleep.

That hypnosis can be a very potent weapon to add to the therapeutic armoury is underlined by the career of James Esdaile, a Dundee surgeon who left his native Dundee to practise in India and who gives his name to the Esdaile state, the deepest state known in hypnosis. Esdaile practised major surgery in India on a large scale for many years before the discovery of anaesthetics. His only anaesthetic was hypnosis. He was both Surgeon and Anaesthetist and used hypnosis for such dreadfully painful procedures as amputations and the removal of bladder stones. Esdaile wrote up 375 cases of major surgery under hypnosis. They were all reported as painless and moreover, although this was the heyday of sepsis, all cases were reported as having healed quickly without much infection. Yet, when he retired from India and began to practise in his hometown of Dundee, he had little success with hypnosis. There was a good reason for this. By this time, ether had already been discovered in Canada and chloroform in Edinburgh. Since these discoveries people no longer felt obliged or motivated to generate – under direction – their own anaesthesia, as it were.

In the story of James Esdaile lies the whole basis of

successful hypnotherapy. If one's patient comes in with a strong motivation to succeed, then that success is very likely. To give an example: if a man comes to a hypnotherapist for help to stop smoking because his own doctor has told him he will die in five years unless he gives up cigarettes, his motivation is strong. If, on the other hand he comes in because his wife has told him she can't stand his smoking a day longer when he himself doesn't want to stop, then he is a much less promising prospect. It is said that the hypnotist should ideally be like a catalyst in a chemical reaction, enabling the reaction to occur without taking too active a part in it and this is more than true. What has always appealed to me most about hypnotherapy is the DIY element. Success, if it occurs, is usually due to patient and therapist in equal measures, but the contribution of the patient is at least as important as that of the practitioner.

Esdaile was probably on a better wicket in the East, since Eastern peoples are by definition more likely to be mystics, and consequently better at self-hypnotism. Successful walking on white hot stones incidentally, as is practised more in the East, is reckoned to be due to a combination of self-hypnosis and the expertise that comes from long practice in putting the foot down for an infinitesimal period on each stone, but it is certainly practised successfully in many places notably perhaps the South Sea Islands, and blistering of the feet does not occur.

Mention of walking on hot stones brings me to another practical example of the uses of hypnotherapy and that is the treatment of burns. As happens frequently in this country, in a general hospital in America there is usually a Burns Unit, which will normally have a hypnotherapist standing by for emergencies. Treatment can be very effective and this is the sequence of events. The symptoms of a burn, that is, what the patient feels, are heat and pain. The signs of a burn, that is, what is visible to the onlooker, are redness and swelling. If the hypnotherapist gets to the patient quickly enough in the early stages after an acute burn, then a state of deep hypnosis produces considerable lessening of the pain and a sensation of cold instead of the acute heat. The result of these changes is not only the greater and more rapid comfort of the patient, but a considerable lessening of the objective signs of the burn, that is the redness and swelling. It is also very likely that the more severe signs such as blistering and breaking of the skin, a slowing down of the healing process and probable scarring will be much mitigated or done away with altogether. This obviously makes hypnotherapy in such circumstances very worthwhile. It also underlines the theme of motivation as brought out in the Esdaile scenario: if you are in intense pain and deep hypnosis will mitigate that pain or do away with it altogether, you have the strongest possible motivation to co-operate.

I was interested to read of a man who was very much in the tradition of James Esdaile but who lived nearly a hundred years later. This was Captain Michael Woodruffe of the Australian Army Medical Corps, Surgeon-in-Charge of a Japanese Prisoner of War Camp Hospital in Singapore with no anaesthetic drugs left.[1]

His 'hospital' had no proper beds, mattresses or sheets, while his operating theatre was a wooden hut with a mud floor. In these primitive surroundings, Captain Woodruffe operated on patients with acute abdominal emergencies and performed amputations. Anaesthetics, both general and local had run out, and the Japanese would allow no more, so a

1 Sir Michael Woodruffe, *Nothing Venture Nothing Win*, (Scottish Academic Press).

colleague suggested he should try unconventional (what today would be called 'alternative') anaesthesia, and as a result he hypnotised his patients.

Over a few months up until the Japanese surrender, several dozen surgical and dental procedures were conducted in this manner. Woodruffe records the case of one man with a severe infection of the hand where the whole of the arm was rendered anaesthetised. Nevertheless the potency of anaesthesia hypnosis was demonstrated just as dramatically here as in Esdaile's series of cases and it appears that the amount of post-operative infection and sepsis in an environment where they obviously abounded was reduced just as dramatically as with James Esdaile. Perhaps this is not so surprising, given the calibre of Michael Woodruffe, for simply to keep one's own morale up in circumstances like a Japanese Prisoner of War Camp, to say nothing of the morale of one's fellows and to save their lives into the bargain demands a most exceptional human being.

And what became of Captain Michael Woodruffe? He ended up as Professor of Surgery at Edinburgh University, and moreover eventually performed the first ever kidney transplant in Britain, an achievement appropriately recognised by a knighthood. I don't know if he received any honour for his surgical work in Singapore, but there is not the slightest doubt in my own mind that he was worthy of a VC.

When practising as a hypnotherapist, I always try to spend some considerable time explaining hypnosis to a patient coming for the first consultation; indeed this is vital, since if they are not well briefed and they don't experience what they expect to experience, they won't be back.

The first and most important thing for them to understand is that at no time will they be asleep, as so many expect. Hypnosis is best defined as a state where the body is progressively relaxed, but the mind remains alert although the critical faculty is dimmed or set in abeyance altogether.

Secondly, and arising from this first point, I stress to the patient that it is they, not myself, who are in control of the situation. If I were to suggest to them something that they didn't want to do or something that went against their principles, they would open their eyes at once and come out of the trance.

Thirdly, the process is almost invariably pleasurable. It is at the same time the most pleasant and the safest treatment in Medicine, as in no way does it depend on drugs. Fourthly, it is relaxing and reassuring in equal amounts. Fifthly, it can transform someone who is shy and reticent into someone with strong self-belief, sometimes quite dramatically. Sixthly, motivation is all-important to success. If you come well-motivated you want to be hypnotised. Seventh, rapport between subject and hypnotist is all-important. Eighth, hypnosis is essentially a dream-state, and usually just as pleasant.

There are certain laws in psychology which are very much applicable in hypnotherapy. Two have particular relevance: the first, the law of reverse effect, lays down that the more you consciously try to achieve something, the more difficult it becomes. In any situation people tend to co-operate more willingly if they are not confronted, not told to do something, and equally this applies in hypnosis: one succeeds much better with a gentler, coaxing approach. The second law is that of direct effect, which states that a stronger emotion will always take precedence over a weaker one. This is applied in hypnotherapy as follows: when trying to change something that has some relevance to emotion, e.g. helping someone to give up smoking, the hypnotist calls to his aid a stronger emotion, e.g. stressing to a mother under hypnosis her love and devotion to her young baby, and how totally vulnerable it is, and how much more vulnerable it would be if anything happened to her. Mother-instinct is so strong that recruiting a stronger emotion like this seldom fails.

Of course, to some extent, the success of otherwise of hypnotherapy depends on the subject. It is probably true to say that very deep hypnotic subjects are born not made, but a lighter one can be turned into a deeper one by several consecutive sessions. Imagination can be a hypnotist's strong ally. To take an extreme example, just picture the workman whom we may have seen sitting on a girder 200 feet or so up in the air, dangling his legs and enjoying his lunchtime sandwiches. There is no way you are going to do this, and certainly no way I am, but if you can be induced, under hypnosis, to see yourself clearly doing this and, more than that, actually acknowledging that you can do it, you have a very much better chance of carrying it out once you have emerged from the hypnosis.

Children from about the age of seven upwards make excellent subjects, usually enthusiastic. They love to have their imaginations involved. When *Star Trek* was in its early days on TV it was a very potent ally. You simply had to suggest to the child that he or she was in front of the TV screen, ask them to close their eyes, watch the Starship Enterprise floating slowly away, getting smaller and smaller in the distance, and they were in hypnosis in no time at all. A young child will stay quite comfortably in hypnosis for half an hour, perhaps wriggling a bit more than his adult counterpart but certainly enjoying the state.

In early childhood conditions, hypnosis is the treatment of choice for a number of conditions most especially bedwetting and migraine. In 1969, when I had recently done an initial weekend's course at the Medical and Dental Hypnosis

Society in Newcastle and was eager to try it out on every possible occasion, I was called out of bed one night to a little boy of five with acute croup. This is always frightening for both mother and child, a condition of rapid and noisy breathing difficulties and such a situation well warrants a night call. Previously, with a child in this state I would have gone straight into my bag for a syringe, injected the child and waited for the breathlessness to quieten down before going back to bed. On this occasion, however, I thought to myself, 'I wonder…' I sat on the bed and began to talk and reassure the little boy in a slow monotone. Very much to my surprise, in about five minutes the child was asleep and the stertor had gone right out of his breathing. Since hypnosis, if left alone, will always become normal sleep I heaved a sigh of relief and went back to bed, much encouraged to go on with it. Ever since then I have looked forward to treating children.

Coming now to some more cases of my own, the first is an example of neurotic illness. In conditions of this nature the cause of the trouble can very often be traced back to childhood and is usually a minor horror story, sometimes a major one to the child; consequently the defence mechanisms in the mind induce the child to shut off the memory so that they are not conscious of it as they grow up and it is buried. Usually in order to bring about a cure you have to take them back, to 'regress' them into childhood and search about, doing some detective work in order to expose the particular relevant buried memory. Once you have found out and exposed the buried memory both under hypnosis and probably in discussion after the session, then it's like letting out a blind boil and the cure is quite quick.

The first case of this nature I have in mind now was a lady of thirty, very normal in every way with one hang-up only: for years she had been unable to go to her own front gate or sit in the garden during the summer, unless her husband was with her, because of her fear of wasps and bees. Regression seemed indicated. I don't normally attempt this until perhaps a third session anyway, as the subject needs preparation. I got her back to five years old when she showed signs of distress and then told me her story.

'I was playing with other little girls in front of my terrace house and we were skipping. There was a sharp corner at the top of the road. Another little girl called out, "Mary, there's a wasp on your neck!" At the same time someone else called out, "Mary, there's a car coming!" '

Mary obviously jumped, unscathed by wasp and missed by car. But always afterwards the two things were compounded in her mind: 'a wasp means death.' Her regression completely cured this.

This second case has a parallel background in that it's another example of one situation compounding another. This one concerned a man of 31 with a very bad stammer. Now it is true that a stammer is one of the hardest things to treat in an adult, even for a Speech Therapist. If the cause in childhood can be tracked down the outlook is much better.

Under hypnosis I narrowed this down to an occasion when William, aged six, was walking home from school with his dad. The short cut which they took was through private grounds so they were in fact trespassing. Suddenly the owner of the land appeared with a big fierce-looking dog. William dashed into the undergrowth and hid. There were two pressing but conflicting needs in his mind – his instincts told him either to scream or to run away. Either course of action would have brought a big fierce dog on top of him. He repressed his natural instincts and stayed still and undetected, but he was left with a stammer from then on. Since this was a horrific experience for a child of six, he had locked it away in the depths of his mind and had no conscious knowledge of it until I regressed him back to that incident.

Having been induced under hypnosis to let go of some of that suppressed emotion, his stammer improved considerably although he hadn't altogether lost it when last I saw him. Stammers incidentally are much more common in boys than in girls but not easy to treat in either sex, often requiring considerable patience.

A third case of mine was very different but equally unusual. It involved a girl, approaching 20, who was a nurse. The problem, which had troubled her for two years, was a total inability to open the fingers of either hand; she had been investigated in hospital by neurologists who thought the condition was probably psychological but could throw no further light on its origins.

The girl herself coped amazingly well, although as she was a good pianist the condition must have been very frustrating for her. However, she had somehow managed to take her driving test during the time in question and had not been off work, contriving to give hypodermic injections regularly, disability or no. She made an admirable impression on me. I couldn't succeed myself in causing any movement when trying to force her fingers apart.

I had three sessions of hypnotherapy with her without making any progress except to bring her a bit deeper into hypnosis each time. I had resolved that in a week's time I would try to regress her to an earlier stage in life to see if that shed any light on the original cause. On the morning of the appointment, a week later, she phoned me to say that the fingers of one hand were relaxing. Should she come in? I said yes and when I saw her, the other hand was beginning to follow suit. I put her straight back into hypnosis and suggested as strongly as I could that the process would go on to complete normality and would stay as such. In fact, this happened very quickly and has remained to date. I still have no clue as to the original cause, but I feel it would be folly now not to let well alone.

Two more cases come to mind, though they are not my own. Number one was recounted by Dr Herbert Spiegel, a New York psychiatrist, at a meeting of the National Society which I attended a few years ago. The subject was a girl in her mid-twenties who belonged to a fairly primitive religious cult in the New York hinterland. She hadn't walked for seven years and no one knew why. Spiegel had been asked to see her because of his eminence in his field. It so happened that he could get away to see her only on a Sunday.

At first her church Elders demurred but then agreed to the Sunday, saying that if he would see her in the church in front of the assembled congregation it would be – if a cure ensued – to the greater glory of the Lord. Spiegel agreed and duly went. He was ushered to a seat on one end of a raised platform above the congregation. The girl was wheeled in at the other end. The atmosphere was fraught. The girl immediately rose from her wheelchair and walked across to him, the first time she had walked in seven years. This illustrates no doubt mixed elements in the cure, with motive, faith and atmosphere all playing a part.

The second was also recounted at a meeting by the President of the American Hypnosis Society, unusually a Professor of both Surgery and Psychiatry, Professor Dabney Ewin from New Orleans. He had been digressing on the use of hypnosis in the treatment of acute burns. As I have already mentioned earlier, in Burns Units in America they have a hypnotist standing by for acute cases. If the patient is quickly hypnotised – and the motive there is very strong to enter hypnosis quickly to escape the acute pain – and suggestion is made of the limb being packed round with ice, the pain will be relieved quickly, the shock mitigated and the subsequent redness and blistering very greatly reduced, healing being speeded up. All this is well proven. Professor Ewin suggested we use it on our own children for sunburn, and in this connection he told a true story.

One weekend he had staying in his house a Catholic priest who had very fair skin and light gingery hair, a type such as I used to have to send home from the Western Desert because they couldn't take the sun. The priest fell asleep by the swimming pool and came in with both legs a fiery red and about to blister. The Professor was away for the weekend but his wife had a good idea of his methods. 'Father,' she said, 'why don't you go up and lie on your bed for three hours until teatime and imagine you are lying beside an icy cool stream and bathing your legs alternately in the running water?'

He came down at teatime still in his shorts. One leg was starting to blister; the other looked quite normal. 'Goodness, Father!' she said, 'Whatever happened?'

'Well,' he replied, 'I got my left leg in quite easily but my right hip is very arthritic and I wasn't able to get the right leg in at all!'

So, hypnotherapy undoubtedly works and is beginning to be accepted as a 'mainstream' medical treatment, but how does it work? Basically, it is largely to do with the fact that we have two halves to our brains and those halves function differently, a concept reflected in the dualism of the Ancient Greeks and the Roman idea of the 'alter ego' which postulated that we often function as two people.

What firmly lifted hypnotherapy finally into the twentieth (and twenty-first) century, and what is gradually dispersing the aura of witchcraft was research by Dr Roger Sperry and his two co-workers Gazzaniga and Levy, who worked with split brain monkeys from 1960 to 1980 and won a Nobel Prize also for their research into the separate hemispheres of the brain. These researches spelled out in detail for the first time the separate functions vested in each hemisphere of the brain. There are many of these functions, so I shall list here only the most important.

There are others but those listed in the table overleaf are the most relevant to hypnosis and the most important of them are to do with time and logic. In respect of time, if you ask someone who has been in hypnosis for twenty minutes how long they have been in that state, they may say anything from three minutes to an hour – 'normal' awareness of time is suspended.

Equally, the subjects of hypnosis will accept suggestions quite uncritically and very often carry them out equally uncritically when restored in due course to another state of consciousness. As a direct result of these researches it has become clear that the hypnotist progressively puts the critical left brain into a state of abeyance, so that he can make direct contact with the more suggestible right brain and therein implant suggestions that might not have been entertained at all if made to the subject's normal logical state of consciousness. In the same way, the hypnotist can draw out from the right brain information, memories etc. which the left brain might be standing guard over in a normal state of consciousness.

The author and poet, Rudyard Kipling, a uniquely gifted man and another Nobel Prizewinner, probably had a real inkling of this notion of two sides to the brain, for in his picaresque novel, Kim at the end of one of the chapters we find the following short poem:

Left hemisphere of the brain is:	**Right hemisphere** of the brain is:
Verbal: using words to name, describe and define.	**Non-verbal**: awareness of things but minimal connection with words.
Logical: drawing conclusions based on one thing following another in logical order.	**Intuitive:** making leaps of insight, often based on incomplete patterns, hunches, feelings or visualisings.
Analytical: figuring things out step by step and part by part.	**Synthetic:** putting things together to form wholes.
Temporal: keeping track of time.	**Non-temporal:** without a sense of time.
Rational: drawing conclusions from reason and facts.	**Not requiring a basis of reason** and factual willingness to suspend judgement.

Much I owe to the lands that grow
  Much to the lives that fed
Give praise to Allah who gave me two
  Separate sides to my head.
Much I reflect on the good and the true
  In the Faiths beneath the sun
Give praise to Allah who gave me two
  Sides to my head, not one.
I could go without shirt or shoe
  Friend, tobacco or bread
Rather than lose for a moment the two
  Separate sides of my head.

Since the state of hypnosis has been proved scientifically to have no relationship to sleep, nor to hysteria, as the famous French neurologist Charcot believed, it emerges at last as an entity in its own right. It has been proved to be simply an altered state of consciousness, not any kind of abnormal state whatsoever, and a state that most people are capable of achieving.

Having now practised regularly for 25 years, I have become increasingly enthusiastic about hypnosis for its ability to reopen doors which have long been closed to orthodox medicine and I wish I had been introduced to it much earlier in my career.

CHAPTER NINE

'Golf – when you shout fore, score six and write down five'

Much of the earlier part of this book has been devoted, in one way or another to my practice of medicine. I want now to give my readers a little glimpse into other facets of my life – hints of which you may already have picked up. There have been three priorities in my life: my family, my patients and my golf. If you were to talk to my wife alone, she might not put them in quite that same order!

In Scottish schools, cricket is seldom compulsory whereas golf is positively encouraged. I started to play at the age of ten at Elie, a favoured Edinburgh resort about twenty minutes from St Andrew's where my grandmother had a little house. Elie was the home town of James Braid, one of the great golfing triumvirate of a hundred years ago, Braid, Vardon, and Taylor. It was Braid who laid out the magnificent King's and Queen's courses at Gleneagles. It was said in Braid's young prime that Elie could have fielded six golfers including Braid himself, who would have defeated any six anywhere in the world. Thirty years or so later, an Elie blacksmith, Nelson Smith, defeated the great Bobby Jones in the first round of the British Amateur.

My grandmother's house was situated at the sixth tee, and when I was a child I could start and finish there without going near the clubhouse and without bothering over any trivial formalities such as green fees – this was probably the start of a lifetime of deceit! Later, my school holidays were spent on the Island of Arran, which boasts about nine golf courses, each one small but each with its own peculiar charm, notably Blackwater Foot, a twelve-holer, the only one I know well. I should like to put in a 'plug' for Arran if you haven't been there. They say it's the Highlands in microcosm – all the beauty and much more accessible. The island abounds in deer and boasts a 2,700-foot mountain, Goat Fell, which is a good climb. Half Arran's charm as a holiday destination lies – or lay at least then – in the fact that families go back year after year for holidays to the same villages, and indeed when I went back after the war with my own family after a gap of about thirty years, many of the same families were still there.

One incident from that holiday is etched on my memory: Blackwater Foot is on the far, west side of the island and to reach it from the car ferry at Brodick on the east means a journey of ten miles along a hill road called the String road, rather as Kipling says, *with a wheel on the edge of the morning and a wheel on the rim of the pit*. I was driving my family back along this road to the ferry at the end of a holiday with a van in front of me and no chance of passing it for the next three or four miles. I watched a rear door of the van open a little and presently a loaf of bread appeared on the road and I ran over it. I blew my horn to alert the driver. Another loaf appeared, then another and another, then both doors opened and a shelf with the rest of the loaves emerged. I was still sitting on my horn but by then I could read the van driver's mind: 'This rude so-and-so isn't going to get past me.' Another shelf of loaves followed and then cakes large and small and finally the cake shelf. There was nothing more until he pulled into his yard at Brodick. I followed him. He had just registered his empty and shelfless van when I appeared. Till then I had imagined that my six years in the Army had completely topped up my vocabulary, but at that point I discovered that it most certainly hadn't!

Back to the subject of golf and my schooldays in Edinburgh. With two open Championship Courses, Muirfield and St. Andrew's not too far away, we had a chance to watch the golfing greats in the middle and late twenties and in those days could, with luck, get jobs as forecaddies to mark where the balls landed. I followed Bobby Jones round Muirfield, in I think 1928 in the British Amateur, and at around the same time Walter Hagen winning the Open.

Hagen changed the face of British golf. In those days, even for an Open at Muirfield, pros were not admitted to the clubhouses and had to change in the car. Hagen would turn up in his chauffeur-driven Rolls Royce, sit on the lawn in front of the main lounge and ostentatiously change his socks and shoes. Hagen was the acknowledged star of his era and a hell-raiser to boot and was very likely to be in a nightclub until 4 a.m. before a Golf Final. Once, someone said to him, 'Your opponent has been in bed already since 11 p.m.'

'Yes,' said Hagen, 'but he's not asleep.'

The Hagen era gave way to the Henry Cotton era, Cotton then being the outstanding world professional golfer. He was the first public schoolboy to make it in the big time, and I saw him at least once at Muirfield. He was the exponent of draw in golf, and all of us aspiring youngsters were hitting the ball out to the right and making it come back to the middle. Nowadays, it's much more the in thing to fade the ball from left to right. In 1938 at St Andrew's I watched Britain beat America in the Walker Cup, a very rare occurrence in those days. On that day I followed Alec Kyle, a Scottish farmer who won his singles comfortably. Much later in my life I had the pleasure of playing with Alec in the British Seniors Championship at Moortown, Leeds.

During my student days I used to holiday for a week in August at St Andrews and play in the Eden, a big amateur tournament, never, it must be said, with too much success, but this began a long association for me with the ancient University City. As you will recall from an earlier chapter, I actually met my wife there in 1939 when we were both on holiday. (Once when I had to make a speech at the British Rotary Annual Championship there, I claimed to have picked her up in the fish-and-chip queue at the badly lit end of South Street, but this was not absolutely true.) In those days I used in passing to look through the picture windows of the Royal and Ancient Golf Club at the demigods inside, never dreaming that in the future I would become one of them. This I did in 1974, having waited ten years to get in. In the event it was worth it, for the R and A has always been free and easy and friendly and one always meets interesting people. Sometimes, one is even lucky enough to be drawn to play with the likes of Henry Longhurst, Peter Allis's predecessor as ace golf commentator, or Lord Whitelaw, an excellent golfer. I remember coming off the last green after a medal, neither of my partners having been known to me before; one of them excused himself as having urgent business and, as I was having a drink later with the other I asked him who our third had been. 'Oh,' he said, 'he's the Chairman of Lloyds.'

The Old Course is unique in every way. If you were to tell a visitor that the Course was all double greens except four, they wouldn't believe you. A considerable folklore attaches to it. One story, reputedly true, is told about the Foreign Secretary of the time, Arthur Balfour. It seems Mr Balfour was playing the short eleventh, perhaps the most famous in the world, and one of the most difficult, with a pronounced slope on the green. He was about to putt and his caddy said to him, 'Aim aboot a yaird, abune the hole and the ba' will come richt roond tae the hole.' Balfour putted – a lamentable effort – and finished as far away again. There was a silence, then one caddy said in a stage whisper to his colleague, 'And those are the buggers who are running the country.'

The Old is unique also in that every Tom, Dick and Harry walks across it, and you are perfectly free to take your dog round and many do, as indeed I myself have often done. There is a rather nice story about the elderly Colonel followed right round by his Scottie. The Colonel was troubled a bit by his prostate and had to disappear into the whins from time to time. Halfway round he asked his caddy, 'What's the score?'

'I dinna ken, Colonel,' replied the caddy, 'but you're twa up on the wee doggie.'

One more reminiscence: pre-war the starter on the Old was Jimmy Alexander, with one arm and a sharp tongue which even Cabinet Ministers got the benefit of if they drove off before he gave the OK. I was standing waiting with a friend to play off when four young men were on the tee, apparently young professionals. The last to play took a lump out of the sacred turf. Jimmy came bounding out of his hut, 'God,' he said, 'are you going to take the whole so-and-so course with you?' Then turning to us he remarked, 'Ca' yon a Professional? He's got a swing like a public-house door!'

My own golfing career has been largely one of frustration and mediocrity. For most of my life I have been an accomplished 'also-ran', a good runner-up. I realised my ambition only twice in my life and that curiously in the same year, when I was 54 years of age. In that year I won the Club Championship, the second round of our Open Scratch

Competition, and came down to one handicap, my lowest ever. The Championship was a last green affair and I managed to beat Jim Bendall, a scratch player who had figured four times in the Final to my once. Some weeks later I was travelling to London by train, and went into the dining car where I was invited by Jim and his then fiancée, Joyce, to join them for lunch. Afterwards I returned to my compartment and Jim told me later that after I had done so, Joyce had said to him, 'What did you go and let a frail old gentleman like that beat you for?'

A couple of weeks later I had an almost mystical experience playing in the annual Open Scratch Competition which attracts amateurs from the South of Scotland and the North of England. This always consists of two rounds played on a Sunday in August. I had had a busy week in the Practice, was about a stone overweight and had promised my wife that this would be the last time I would ever play two rounds in one day. My son Hugh and a couple of his friends were down to play from Edinburgh University. When I got in at lunch, I had a goodish score of 75 and a pain in my chest. A little lunch and a gin and a tonic and it felt better, so I went out again in the afternoon, caddied for by my daughter, Celia, who had taken over from my wife. The first eight holes I played well, playing in a three ball, one of whom was Jimmy Hastings, a Scottish International and medical colleague. After the eighth Jimmy, who wasn't playing well, said he was packing in. By now I was in more severe pain, and I would dearly have liked to follow suit but I could hardly desert my other partner. The upshot of this was that as I got worse my golf got better and I finally struggled off the eighteenth with a gross 70 which won the second round, unquestionably the best round of my life – and three hours later I was in the Infirmary with a coronary thrombosis! I count my blessings: I was expertly treated and am still lucky enough to be playing regularly 30 years later. Never since, however, have I played more than eighteen holes, or by now I would have joined the ever-swelling ranks of the Divorced.

One more story, a true one that appealed to me: Tom Weiskopf, former Open Champion, came into the crowded lounge of the *Grey Walls Hotel* by Muirfield, and spotted an attractive lady. Stretching out his 6 foot 3 inch frame by her feet he began to chat her up. 'Do you play golf?'

'No, I don't, but my father was quite keen at one time.'

'What did your father do?' Slight pause.

'He was the King of England.'

The lady in question was, of course, Princess Margaret.

Some years ago I wrote for a medical journal, *Pulse,* a tongue-in-cheek piece entitled 'More than your life's worth?' about the hidden dangers to health of playing golf. Its subheading was 'Spending a relaxing couple of hours round a golf course this weekend? Better heed Dr George Jolly's warning before you do.' I reproduce that article here:

Golf: the Darker Side

In the text books, under the headings for specific diseases there is a paragraph headed Etiology, which, incidentally, seems to get shorter with the passage of the years. This paragraph should frequently include, but doesn't, one more word – a four-letter one – golf.

One should not, I hasten to say at the outset, write of the effect on health of golf in a purely pejorative way. There are undoubted benefits. Has not a well-known writer on the sport said that waiting to drive off the first tee at Atlanta, Georgia, is a most effective laxative?

It has been thought in the past that the leisurely amble round that the game affords is of benefit to osteoarthritic joints, and this must be conceded in early cases. However, it should be noted in passing that over-taxation on the tee can put pressure on the body which may distort the little dress-sense golfers possess, whilst success on the green may bring on a frenzied war dance.

It is the purpose of this article to consider the pathology of the game. Golf has a behind-the-scenes role in many illnesses, somatic and psychosomatic, which the medical profession does not, or does not choose to, identify. Under the former heading the commonest lesion is peptic ulcer. From the moment he or she pays the entrance fee, the aspiring golfer is beset by worry. A single-figure handicap once reached, the worry has intensified.

At this stage the gastric acidity has peaked. Added to this it will have become customary when contemplating a long putt to light a cigarette, the latter being fully smoked by holing-out time. It is little wonder that our major golf tournaments are sponsored by Benson and Hedges, Piccadilly and the like. It is only a matter of time before the Citrus Open in Florida is joined by the Cimetidine Open at Cypress Point!

Oesophagitis and hiatus hernia are not far behind. Take a typical case history. This is the Saturday golfer who finishes work at midday in a dilemma. Shall he go home to a rushed cold lunch and colder wife or shall he go straight up to the Club for a sandwich and join his fourball for the inevitable pre-game four rounds of gin, the last one drunk almost neat as its buyer maintains there is enough tonic left from before and is too mean to buy more? Either way he is over a barrel and gastric reflux is inevitable.

'Do you play golf?' Bobby Jones, it must be remembered, couldn't eat and lost pounds during each tournament. He gave the game up at 28 and yet he had a good deal less to worry about in his swing than you have.

Myocardial infaction has a high incidence in golfers in the early 50s, scoring in the high 80s. A typical case history features the victim who comes in after 18, has tea and three double Scotches, and, so restored, is persuaded into another nine when he is neither qualified by training nor morphology for extra time. He has a tendency to succumb at the top of the hill on the third fairway after dragging up his allotted 14 clubs and their huge container (the poorer the golfer the more impressive his impedimenta!).

It is not possible, in a short article, to catalogue the under-cover role that golf plays in physical illness, like the spiro-chaete of old. One must pass to the psychopathology. I do not propose to dwell on those conditions which leap most quickly to mind where golf may play a part in the cause. One thinks at once of acute dementia, suicide, self-mutilation and coprolalia (the compulsive shouting out of obscene words).

Less obvious, and revealed only by very careful history, is the individual, previously of good moral character who, in his early golfing history, has found his ball lying very tight in a Plantain root and, requiring wood to reach the green, has nudged it into a better lie. This often proves a trigger for subsequent shoplifting and, in extreme cases, international fraud.

Golf is no respecter of sex. All the conditions I have mentioned occur also in the female. There are additional symptom complexes, psychological and physical, secondary to the behaviour of the male. The commonest perhaps is the so-called Summer Evening Syndrome, where the male partner, when he should be occupied in preliminary love-play in the long twilight in the summer-house, is in fact on the practice ground. This may lead to frigidity, delayed orgasm, metropathia haemorrhagia and, in severe cases, hysterectomy.

It has been written by no less an authority than Arnold Palmer's father that golf is played from the shoulders up. So many of its adverse effects are made manifest, alas, far away indeed from the scapula.

Playing golf, how often do we feel like imitating the memorable San Francisco millionaire quoted by Alistair Cooke; the millionaire was a dogged old golfer, who pulled his drive, topped his wooden shot, fluffed in the bunker, and took a small divot on the putting green. He straightened up and looked at his more expert companions in utter amazement. 'What am I doing?' he cried, 'I don't have to do this – I'm a rich man!'

My 'home' golf course and club is of course Carlisle, and here we are lucky for in Carlisle Golf Club we have a very attractive and challenging course which, were it in the Surrey stockbroker belt, would be very well known (and much more expensive). Carlisle Golf Club brings me to my last golfing memory and to my final story.

My last memory is, you might say, golfomedical. Close on thirty years ago I used to attend a lad of around ten who had haemophilia, and would have to be sent into hospital for injections of coagulant to stop his severe episodes of bleeding. These were sometimes into joints like the knee joint and we wondered if he would be left with any resultant deformity. He was then a bit puny and undersized. On retiring from Practice, I lost touch with John but occasionally wondered how he had turned out, as he had always met his limitations very gamely.

Then about five years ago I was playing in a four ball at Carlisle Golf Club and on the seventh tee we asked two young men, quicker than we were, to play through. The second to drive, tall and elegant, hit the ball far down the fairway. I complimented him. He said, 'You don't know me, do you?' When I confirmed that I didn't, he just had time to say the word 'haemophilia', and went on his way. My doubts were laid to rest.

And my final story too has links (if you'll pardon the pun) with Carlisle Golf Club: almost 40 years ago, in 1963, I played a very minor role in an incident in which, with hindsight, I should have loved to say I took a leading part. The occasion was Carlisle Golf Club's annual dinner dance, an event which was held in the Ballroom of the *Crown and Mitre Hotel* and which was, you must understand, in those days a very dressy affair. That year's Captain was Bill Berry, a forthright Yorkshireman who liked to back his words with action, and I was his Vice-Captain.

Someone came to our table with the news that a member had brought into the Ballroom four rather long-haired young men and a girl who were not official guests and were not wearing evening dress. Bill said to me, 'I think, George, that these people should be asked to leave.'

I said, 'Yes, Bill, I agree.'

'I'll go and do it myself straightaway,' continued Bill, suiting the action to the words, and returning five minutes later to announce to the table that the deed had been done and the culprits had left without demur.

I have kept to this day the account of the incident, which appeared in a local paper and focused on the young woman involved, and is therefore headed, understandably enough, *Helen Ordered Out as she does the Twist*. Knowing what I know now, I wish I had had the title role in that little drama – it's not everyone who can say that they successfully banished The Beatles and Helen Shapiro from a function of any kind! The Beatles themselves, incidentally, are merely mentioned in passing as 'the Beatles singing group' though the report makes much of the fact that they were wearing leather jackets.

CHAPTER TEN

More of Carlisle, her Citizens and her Institutions

So we move in my reminiscences from Carlisle Golf Club to Carlisle itself and the denizens thereof. Looking back, I well remember a man I never met, though many of my fellow citizens did and were grateful for the encounter. The man in question was George Long, more commonly known as Geordie Long. He was a bonesetter, the name given to osteopaths without degrees or diplomas who practised in former times and he was undoubtedly a very good one.

I never met him, because in earlier days the rules of the General Medical Council precluded me as a doctor from referring a patient to someone like George since he was unqualified. Nonetheless, he was a busy man, something of a genius and a very successful one. He practised up a Close in Caldewgate (where once Robert Burns, no less, was had up before the Magistrate for illegal parking, which in the poet's case consisted of tying up his horse for too long in a busy public thoroughfare. Conditions in Caldewgate have probably not changed too much since that time anyway.) A skilled osteopath, whether he has a degree or not, is born, not made, and the skill dwelling in Geordie's hands saved many an individual from a great deal of prolonged and unnecessary pain had he sought help from more orthodox channels.

At the other extreme were one or two bonesetters who were as bad as Geordie was skilled, but who still seemed to have a following – among the farming community especially, as I discovered when I left a busy consulting hour one afternoon to go and visit a farmer. It transpired that his injury had occurred in the early morning and he had visited a less skilled bonesetter than the aforementioned Geordie. I found him with a bad Potts fracture of the ankle, severe and with much displacement of the bones, but the only treatment afforded him by the rogue bonesetter had been a piece of ordinary sticking-plaster. Moreover, the patient required two weeks in hospital.

The next Carlisle character, stored with pleasure in my memories of my early days here is Monsignor Smith, the senior Roman Catholic priest in Carlisle. He had a wonderful, dry sense of humour and was always good to listen to at dinners. One of his many stories has stayed with me to this day. He recounted how he was walking in one of the parks when he came across a man sitting on a bench, absorbed in his newspaper. He said to him, 'Are you a Roman Catholic?'

'No', said the man.

'Are you a Presbyterian?'

'No', said the man.

'Are you a Methodist?'

'No', said the man.

'Well, what are you?'

The man looked up from his newspaper and said, 'I'm a Quaker. Bugger thee.'

The most distinguished policeman we ever had here was Frank Williamson. He came from Manchester where he was a Detective Chief Superintendent and I met him at the end of the day he had arrived for interview, which had been both busy and stressful. It fell to me to give him the medical examination for the job and I remember him looking so part worn that I took a bottle I kept in my cupboard and gave him a stiff dram. He passed the examination all right. A dedicated policeman, his first thought was always his men, and a number of overdue promotions were made shortly after his arrival.

Frank Williamson did not stay very long with us, however. That was in no way a reflection on any shortcoming of his, far from it in fact: he was very soon on the way up. He became Chief Constable of Cumbria. I think, looking back, he was the last Chief Constable that Carlisle ever had and from that time onwards the senior police officer in Carlisle was a Chief Superintendent who in turn answered directly to Carleton Hall. Frank Williamson did not long remain Chief Constable of Cumbria. He was moved to London right to the top of the tree as HM Inspector of Constabulary.

And now to move from individuals to an institution. When I first came to Carlisle in 1947 I joined the Border Club, partly because it was only three doors away from my Surgery premises in Portland Square. The Border Club, which eventually amalgamated with another to become the Border and County Club remained very popular until the time when the breathalyser began to bite; after that it was never the same again. When I first joined the members fell into two main groups, the younger element who would be in the Club at 6 o'clock in the evening or thereabouts to unwind for half an hour on the way home from work to their ever-loving. Those in the second category were for the most part retired and tended to spend a good deal more of the day there, particularly as throughout its active life it purveyed an excellent lunch at a very reasonable price, thanks to a very dedicated staff. The breathalyser really strangled such clubs by degrees, as they could not subsist on lunchtime takings alone. The Club struggled on until July 1996 and then, to our sorrow, folded. I'd like to tell you a story about it in its better days.

This story brings in the Crichton Royal Hospital in Dumfries where in earlier days patients of reasonable means with liquor problems went from near and far to be dried out in comfort. At the time of which I'm writing, three Border Club members were all there together, including the Chairman. A fourth member, not so incarcerated, got into his car out of a sense of Christian duty, and drove to Dumfries to visit them. He was ushered into the room where they were sitting together whereupon they rose to a man, and said with one voice, 'How very nice to see you here Ray – now we'll have a Bridge four.'

From a medical institution to a medical individual, this time a lady, Bella Moore. Bella was a nursing sister, certainly the best known in the Cumberland Infirmary. When she died a year or so ago, the Crematorium was packed out. Bella was a marvellous nurse, and an extrovert like her boss, the late Dr Tommy Studdert, with a good command of the English language. In the later part of her career she was promoted away from the battlefield as it were, to an administrative job which she hated. In the present scheme of things this happens to too many dedicated nurses, who are completely wasted in such posts. I had the pleasure of being nursed by her in 1969 and I'm sure I recovered more quickly because of it. I remember having strolled in to chat to the occupant of the next cubicle who had just been admitted that day. Sister Moore came bustling in and said to the Probationer Nurse already there, 'Is that any way to make a bloody bed?' She did not know, as I did, that the new occupant of the bed was none other than the Archdeacon of Carlisle! Fortunately, as anyone who knew and loved Charley Nurse – and so many did – could have told her, he wouldn't have given a toss.

Another citizen, better known than most by reason of the office he held, is Jimmy Stables, OBE. Jimmy was Clerk to the Magistrates and succeeded better than any in holding the balance between the Bench and the wrongdoers, making sure that the former did not exceed their powers and defending the rights of the underdog at the same time. These duties he performed with splendid impartiality. As Police Surgeon, I spent a good deal of time in his Court and have reason to be grateful for his kindness in making my life as easy as possible: I had often to spend time waiting to be called in Court and he minimised this for me as much as he could. I was always grateful too for his ever-ready sense of humour and his ability to deal effectively with the pompous and the pedantic.

While on the subject of the Law, I would like to slip in another true little story. This concerned a senior Police Officer in the city force who moved into the country to live. On one occasion, he came up to the Golf Club with a Police Golf outing and was sitting at the Bar chatting to the Club Secretary who asked him how he was enjoying life in the country. 'Splendid', he said, 'it's been a wonderful spring and I've had daffodils growing on my property as far as the eye could see. I took them down to the Market week after week and they sold very well. The taxman will know nothing about it.' The Secretary of the Golf Club, to whom he was talking, just happened also to be the taxman!

One more outstanding citizen whom I got to know better and better as the years went past, since we were next-door neighbours, was Mick Potts. Mick was an Accountant by training, the son of a textile manufacturer, who joined the business in due course and helped it prosper for many years until financial events in the country caught it in a squeeze and it folded. Later, largely through his efforts, a new business rose like a phoenix from the ashes and, fostered by Mick and his sons, it became international. That was Mick's daytime career. After dark, he was the very versatile leader of the Gateway Jazz Band and this in due course took him into the highest audiences in the land. His wife, Anne, liked to tell the story of the day the phone rang at home and a voice said, 'This is Buckingham Palace.'

She was about to say, 'Pull the other one', but she thought better of it and didn't – which was just as well as it was, indeed, Buckingham Palace.

I am, sadly, not musical, so I couldn't properly assess Mick's gifts in that direction, but I am assured that he was quite outstanding on both piano and trumpet, and his three sons inherited his musical prowess, Adrian and Matthew on the piano and Simon on the drums.

In addition to these gifts, Mick was as clever an after-dinner speaker as I ever heard in this town and constantly a witty conversationalist and companion. It wasn't in his nature to spare himself by day or by night and he would arrive home in the evening, having driven almost the length of England, in time to turn out for an engagement. This punishing lifestyle together with the loss a few years earlier of his lovely wife, Anne, hastened his own premature death. The Gateway Jazz Band played at his funeral.

As I was writing this section, the name of Professor Charnley cropped up in discussion. I suppose about 25–30 years ago Professor Charnley was a pioneer, if not *the* pioneer of hip replacement in England. He operated in Wrightington Hospital near Parbold, which in turn is near Wigan, so about as far away as it could be from being a seat of learning. It just goes to prove what the poet says:

Full many a gem of purest ray serene,
The dark unfathomed caves of ocean bear …

A number of patients went from Carlisle to have hip replacements, which were done most expertly considering the early stage of research that the operation was at. I am reminded of a particular instance involving a patient of mine, whose name was Tommy Norman, an elderly gentleman, over 70 (well, I regarded him as elderly then, though I wouldn't now). Tommy had been on the waiting list for this operation for a long time, but at last his name came up and he was despatched by ambulance from Carlisle for admission to the hospital to be operated on the next day by the Professor. He got there, but because of some technicality they were unable to operate on him then and equally unable to admit him overnight because of a lack of beds (this whole story has a curiously modern ring, don't you think?). The ambulance set off back for Carlisle, the patient mildly disappointed but taking it with good grace as always. A little way down the road the ambulance driver asked him, 'Tommy, would you like a little bit of excitement?' Tommy replied in the affirmative so they put on their flashing lights and their sirens on the motorway and brought him all the way back to Carlisle at about 85 miles per hour. The exhilaration of the journey, he told me, largely counteracted the disappointment. I seem to remember that he was successfully operated on a couple of weeks or so later.

CHAPTER ELEVEN

The Pen is Mightier than the Syringe

I have had a love affair with poetry for most of my life. Having been unfortunate enough to be born without an ear for music, yet ever in search of beauty of sound, poetry was the best substitute.

As you may recall from the first chapter, when I was six years old my father used to come into my bedroom before I went to sleep and read to me the *Rubaiyat of Omar Khayyam*. I hadn't the remotest idea what this paean of praise to the virtues of eating, drinking and being merry for tomorrow we die was about, but the sheer grace and beauty of its quatrains got through to me even at that age – as they still do.

I have been writing verse for most of my adult life, some of which is reproduced later in this book, but I have never succeeded in eliminating the vein of cynicism which keeps breaking through – not that lyric poetry is very fashionable any more.

Associating verse with the medical profession has set me thinking. The only outstanding example of a poet-cum-doctor, and at his best there is no finer, is John Keats who had a medical training at Guy's Hospital before going on to die in Rome of consumption aged just 26, but with a wonderful output of poetry behind him.

Examples of doctors-turned-authors are much thicker on

the ground. Probably the leading modern exponents of the species were A. J. Cronin and Somerset Maugham. Cronin probably remained the more faithful to his profession, producing such bestsellers of book and screen as *The Citadel* and *Dr Finlay's Casebook*. (I enjoyed the first TV series of the latter very much, by the way, but I couldn't be doing with the repeat. How about you?)

Incidentally, I remember reading a family biography of Somerset Maugham called *Somerset and all the Maughams* by his brother Lord Maugham, the High Court Judge. It mentioned the small beck that runs alongside the seventeenth green at Carlisle Golf Club, a burn into which most of us have put a ball with irksome regularity. That beck is mentioned in the book because it is called the Pow Maughan and it seems that in early days the Maugham family, which came from the Appleby district, very often spelt their name, Maughan as in Pow Maughan and Lord Maugham in his book saw fit to dignify that beck with a mention.

Unfortunately, Carlisle cannot boast a truly medical author turning out adventure and mystery novels. Probably the nearest we get to it is George McDonald Frazer, a journalist by profession, but brought up in the medical practice of his father, Dr Willy Frazer, and of Dr Alan Frazer who was, I always believed, although I am not certain of this, Willy's brother.

George McDonald Frazer early on wrote a local classic, *The Steel Bonnets*, about the Border Reivers, and later the series of *Flashman* novels which were hugely successful on stage and screen. I was introduced to the first of these in 1969 when I happened to be suffering from a heart attack in the Infirmary just three cubicles along from Willy Frazer who kindly sent along for me to read the first of the *Flashman* series, hot off the press. I enjoyed this greatly because it took as its subject the Afghan Campaign of 1842 where the British Expeditionary Force lost every woman and child and every man but one of the Expedition, all slaughtered by the Afghans on their retreat from Kabul. I found it fascinating because it put flesh on the bones of my ignorance of that period of history.

Perhaps the most successful medical author of our time is Dr Richard Gordon, who wrote the *Doctor in the House* books, another series as successful on the screen as on paper. I had the good fortune to meet him once: the medical journal *Pulse* staged a literary competition open to all the doctors in the country, with a very wide choice of entry material. Although I didn't win the competition, I was runner-up, and you will find my entry reproduced in this book – the *Tomlinson* excerpt. Part of the prize was a weekend in a London hotel with a luncheon where the prizes were presented by Dr Richard Gordon, and I was lucky enough to get a seat beside him. He had actually qualified as an anaesthetist but had decided that the grass was greener on the literary side of the fence and no doubt made a large fortune. He was a pleasant and most entertaining man who had recently returned from a trip to America. He said there he had met a lady gynaecologist who told him she had thought of a way of teaching male doctors not to do rough pelvic examinations on women. She proposed that as part of his training, every gentleman medical student (if that is not a contradiction in terms) should be taken into a cubicle and stripped, then submitted to the indignity of lithotomy stirrups (all too familiar, alas, to lady patients). After an interval a strange female doctor would walk into the room, and, in the words of the lady gynaecologist, 'Squeeze his balls and leave without saying a word.'

The trouble is, as Richard Gordon pointed out, the medical

student might enjoy it!

Although my own literary efforts can scarcely be compared to the aforementioned authors', my own strongest interest, even when I was embarking on a medical career was and probably still is English, but I thought that if I studied English I would probably end up teaching and I never reckoned myself a particularly good teacher. To compensate for what I missed in the world of literature I have very much enjoyed writing articles and verse right through my career, most of which never got much further than the medical press.

When it comes to reading literature, and especially poetry, I have always been a great fan of Scotland's National Bard, Robert Burns, and have spoken periodically at Burns' Nights for the past 50 years or so. (On a recent 25 January, I quoted a patient of mine who said to me, 'You Scots doctors are a bit like haemorrhoids. If you come down and go back it's not so bad. If you come down and stay down, you're a pain in the proverbial.')

Burns' achievements and his legacy of verse were quite remarkable.

> Let Kings and Courtiers rise and fa'
> This world has mony turns
> But brightly beams abune them a'
> The star o' Robby Burns.

When we consider that he did hard physical work, lived only to the age of 38 and wrote mostly by candlelight, his output was extraordinary. The fact that he would never kowtow to authority and constantly wrote such scathing things as these four lines about the Hanoverian Royal Family of his time:

> The injured Stuart line is gone
> A race ignoble sits their throne

An idiot race to honour lost
Who know them best despise them most.

did not endear him to the Establishment. Perhaps it's not therefore surprising that he doesn't have a Gothic monument in Princes Street like the more mundane Scott or a column in St Andrew's Square like Dundas, a contemporary of Burns and Scottish Secretary – not to mention virtual dictator of Scotland in Burns' time. Dundas, a bitter enemy of the poet's, but a close drinking companion of Pitt, was created Lord Melville. Yet Robert Burns is the only man of these islands whose birth is celebrated worldwide and the rites observed on such occasions give universal pleasure. It has been suggested that if one man should be nominated as the Man for the Millennium for these islands, Burns must be a strong candidate. There can be few men who brought so little into the world and left so many parts of it so much enriched – all in the space of a relatively short life, a life which, moreover, he continually endangered by fearlessly speaking out for free speech and the common man, establishing himself in the process as Scotland's finest lyric poet!

Nevertheless, it must be said that Burns made as sure as he could that his own line would not die out.... I am sure that, had he been blest enough to live in the age of the contraceptive pill he would have written an Ode to it, but since he didn't, I wrote one for him.

Robert Burns addresses The Pill

Wee modest, sugar-coatit pill
Oh, what a magic lies intill
Thy bosom – for thou sound'st the knell
  O'ovulation
And gi'est a wee bit extra thrill
  Tae fornication.

Thou bonny gem by man designed
To soothe the suffering o' mankind
To ease the body, free the mind
  Frae repercussion
Adorn and comfort womankind
  Jap, Scot or Russian.

How better I could reconcile
Poetic licence and lifestyle
Had I met thee – restored the smile,
  And quelled the dither
In Bonny Mary o'Argyle
  And mony anither.

And a' my tumbles around Galloway
Would still have left them in a fallow way
And kept the bonny wee things all away
  Frae bodily taint
And I'd sit in the Kirk o'Alloway
  A very Saint!

It has always grieved me that Burns lived before the limerick became popular, because his flashing wit would doubtless have turned out some very good ones. The nearest he came, I think, to the spirit of the limerick, was in his epitaphs to friend or foe alike, where he excels. My favourite of these is this one written on a deceased schoolmaster in Mauchline.

Lament him Mauchline husbands a'
  He aften did assist ye
For had ye bidden lang awa'
  Your wives wad ne'er hae missed ye.

Ye Mauchline bairns as by ye pass
  Tae school in bands tegither
Oh tread but lightly on his grass
  He micht have been yer feyther!

And this leads me on to the limerick itself. I have always enjoyed the classic ones, and have spent much leisure time in writing them when I might have been doing more gainful things. The art of the good limerick is to make it tantalisingly insinuating without being overtly rude. It has been said that:

The Limerick is furtive and mean
You must keep her in close quarantine
  Or she's off to the slums
  And as quickly becomes
Disorderly, drunk and obscene.

Many famous people have tried their hands at the limerick. The one that follows here is attributed to President Woodrow Wilson of the USA whose wife apparently had Carlisle connections and is (or was) commemorated by a plaque at the top of Lowther Street. Woodrow Wilson wrote:

I sat next to the Duchess at tea
It was just as I feared it would be
  Her rumblings abdominal
  Were truly phenomenal
And everyone thought it was me.

The medical word for such rumblings, by the way, is the wonderfully onomatopoeic *borborygmi*, a word, I think, which couldn't express better what it is meant to express! The two following limericks are my own; the first was a winner in a literary competition in Punch. We were given the last word of each line and had to fit a limerick round it.

A common young lady from Goole
Went to Hull to a Finishing School
  Now her accent redone
  She can pass off as one
From the West End of West Hartlepool.

And the second won me a bottle of champagne from a medical newspaper. In this case we were given the first line.

After midnight an old lady phoned,
'I can't sleep; I can't sleep,' she moaned
So I said, 'Honours even,
Just be like St Stephen –
Or myself for that matter – get stoned.'

I'll let you off with two more. Both of these are classics.

There was a young lady of Wantage
Of whom the Town Clerk took advantage
Said the Borough Surveyor,
'Of course you must pay her –
You've altered the line of her frontage!'

And this last one is a valid comment on the scheme of things as we know it today.

A surly and pessimist Druid
A defeatist if only he knew it,
Said, 'The world's on the skids
And I think having kids
Is a waste of good seminal fluid.'

CHAPTER TWELVE

A Chapter of Verse

As I mentioned in the last chapter, one of my chief interests and diversions during the course of my medical career has been writing light verse, often in response to literary competitions in Punch or medical journals. I'm pleased to say that several of the following were winners. You will notice too that, as I also mentioned in the last chapter, many of these do have a somewhat cynical streak! Most of these appeared in the magazine *Hobbydoctor,* to whose editor I am grateful for permission to reproduce them here.

DR BEN ADAM

with apologies to Leigh Hunt

Dr Ben Adam, may his List increase,
In Life's high summer, kind, beloved of all,
Dreaming one night in unaccustomed peace,
Woke with a start to yet another call.
This time, alas, 'twas not Miss Archer's pain
As oftentimes before disturbed the Sleeper,
Nor Jack Hogg, drunk, thumping his wife again,
Tonight a different Caller! 'Twas the Reaper!

Saint Peter met him warmly at the Gate:
'Good Doctor, kindly tell me in what fashion
You lived. And were your good deeds small or great,
To help me in preparing your Citation?'
Ben Adam smiled and slowly made reply,
'I worked,' said he, 'sans glamour and sans fuss.
I'm here because demand outstripped supply:
Write me as one who loved the NHS.'

The Saint half smiled, the morrow dawned, and when
He wakened up to joy and ecstasy,
And read Celestial Orders, Dr Ben
Beheld, writ on the Detail for the Day,
Of kindred souls immortalised, a List,
Those newly come to Paradise that must
Consult the Heavenly Psychiatrist,
And Lo! Ben Adam's name led all the rest!

GHOSTS

It was Christmas Day in the Surgery,
Silent the Waiting-Room,
A dim-lit Tabernacle
With an aura of hurt and doom.

From the picture above the Mantel
Sad-eyed, symbolic sheep
Gazed out on a twilit Chamber –
None there to complain or weep.

But lo! The crepuscular shadows
Suffuse with unearthly glow
And the room for a moment's peopled
With the Ghosts of long ago.

'I died', said a gentle Spirit
With a reminiscent moan,
'Of Agranulocytosis
Due to Phenylbutazone.'

'I', said another sadly,
'Had my earthly tenure closed,
By acute appendicitis,
Alas, undiagnosed.'

'My passing', said a lady,
'Unerringly was fated
From the time he put on forceps
With the cervix undilated.'

'Four-minute consultations,
   How could he understand?
I,' said a woeful Phantom,
   'I died at my own hand.'

Up spoke a wild-eyed Spectre
   With an unearthly sigh,
'Their Family Practitioner
   Alackaday! 'Twas I.

'But Nature in her wisdom
   Is swift to make redress
I died from all these patients'
   Inconsiderateness!'

PSYCHIATRISTS, BLESS THEM ALL

On Monday my receptionist
Showed in a Mr Cramb
I hadn't really known before
Who didn't give a Damn.
I looked him over carefully,
Prescribed Nitrazepam.

On Tuesday he was back again –
He looked at me and wham!
His manner became hostile;
I thought, 'I'm in a jam.'
I changed his medication,
Gave him Medazepam.

Wednesday he shook his fist at me
Just like a battering ram
I called on all the faiths I knew,
Christian, Buddhist, Islam;
With shaking hand I wrote a script
For Tabs. Flurazepam.

On Thursday he insulted me
Called me charlatan and sham,
Just missed my left parietal
With a well-aimed tin of Spam.
I thought, 'I'll fix you good my friend,'
There's still Oxazepam.

On Friday I was sitting my
MRCP exam
But vis-à-vis the papers
My senses fairly swam;
I had to tranquilise myself
With Caps. Lorazepam.

I diagnosed him Saturday,
Said I, 'He's off his trolley, him,'
Completely altered my approach
And ceased therewith to jolly him.
Thought I, 'There's still Diazepam,
No, damn, I'll give him Valium!'

Never saw him again.

MEASURE FOR PLEASURE

'A few more questions, Mr Good,
Have you discomfort after food?

'No?' Then, with hindsight, rashly, I think,
'Tell me what happens when you drink.'

He said, 'When I drink Bells
My abdomen swells.

'When I drink Chivas Regal
I get high as a seagull.

'Every time I drink Bourbon
My thoughts are disturbin'.

'If I drink Black Label
I'm not always able.

'But when I drink Glen Grant
I most certainly can't.

'Yet a good stiff Red Hackle
Makes my chromosomes crackle.

'And a double McKenzies
Sends me into frenzies.

'If I drink Standfast
I find I get canned fast.

'Then when I drink Teachers
I see frightening creatures.

'And a small Isle of Jura
Makes my diction impurer.

'When I drink Claymore
I say more and sway more.

'But give me The Glenlivet
And I'm right as a trivet.

'My wife drinks 100 Pipers
And sometimes I swipe hers.'

MONDAY MORNING IN THE SURGERY

Why Mr Duncan
Your eyes are sunken
Could be your drunken
Saturday night is
Causing gastritis?
Have a week off!

Poor Mrs Sorrell
You've had a quarrel –
He's been immoral,
Your husband Jacob?
And he wants to make up?
Have a week off!

Ah, Mrs Barrell
With little Carol
She's quite catarrhal?
So's Fred and Karen?
And Baby Darren
Has a wee cough?

Mr McKeating
Your constant beating
Is fast depleting
Your wife's stamina.
Why not stop hammering her?
Take a week off.

Lady Whinlatter
Your incessant chatter
Drives your only daughter
To oppobrium.
So take these Nobrium
And a week off.

You walk on hot coals
In your stage act, Miss Knowles?
You've chilblains on the soles
Of both your feet
When away from the heat
In your week off?

Forgive me, Miss Hall
I've an urgent call
From Lauren Bacall.
I must catch the schooner
To Tristan da Cunha
For a week off.

SAPPHICS

As the early sun's rays strike her bedroom windows
Stirs into wakefulness Mrs Walters
'How may I utilise this new day to torment my
NHS doctor?'

Shall I straightaway reach out an elegantly manicured
Hand and lift up that modern boon the telephone,
Ask him in honeyed tones, would he call on his way
In to the Surgery?

Would it perchance cause him more inconvenience
Were I to withhold my fire until coffee time,
Courteously request a visit at the very start
Of his morning list?

In my boudoir surely three quarters of an hour
Spent among satins and scent of Estee Lauder
Must from the man's mind drive unworthy thoughts of
His quaint capitation fee!

Later on, at sundown, at the sherry-party I'll
Glass-in-hand vouchsafe him a replay of symptoms
Forgetting that to meet such situations the Phoenicians
Invented money.'

Not too bad a bargain, when you come to weigh it up.
Elegantly gift-wrapped, an annual compendium
Of skill and solicitude, materials and the workman's time
For three quid odd!

BALLAD OF A FRUSTRATED GP

I think I'll misconduct myself today –
I get so tired of acting ethical
I'll have three G and T's at breakfast time and fall
Flat on my face in Morning Surgery.
This very afternoon I'll make a play
And more, for youngish, nubile Mrs Paul,
Scented, provocative, décolletée
And eager as the Darling Buds of May –
I think I'll misconduct myself today.

I think I'll misconduct myself today –
It's time I broke my Hippocratic Oath;
I'll advertise my charm or skills or both
In soft seductive words to lure astray
The Patient from his chosen Quack away.
I'll fight accepted practice nail and tooth;
It's more than time I met the GMC,
Release the tide that surges inside me –
I think I'll misconduct myself today.

Prince, if you'll vouchsafe to me the key
Of your Zenana where in beauty lie
Your sloe-eyed wives, forgetting my MD
I think I'll misconduct myself today!

IF

by Kipling's GP

If you can treat above a score of patients
   Before two tedious hours have come and gone,
Stalling the while on numerous occasions
   The importunities of the telephone.

If you can sit, a well-intentioned spider
   Incumbent of a stretched and tenuous web
And deal alike with gentleman, outsider,
   Malingerer, hypochondriac or scab.

If you'll preside, a shabbier Solomon
   Kind, courteous, dispassionate of mood,
Rapt but inscrutable, and follow man
   Up hill, down dale, through each vicissitude.

If you'll remind yourself he's only human,
   Be his behaviour never so bizarre
Only outdone by that of sister woman
   Tho' both expect you to be something more.

If you'll receive the younger Rep with courtesy,
   With coffee, outstretched hand and bonhomie,
And never say a single word that hurts, he
   Won't realise you are due on the first tee!

If you'll prescribe his favoured Beta-blocker
   And read his extract from the BMJ
'Mong all he woos you'll be his Lady Docker
   A beacon shining in a world astray.

If you can wear your Cinderella garb
  Unenvying colleagues in the EEC
And still remain essentially a sahib
  Content, with undistorted ECG.

If you can stand, for forty harassing years
  The oafishness of the DHSS
You'll be, at last, transcending blood and tears
  The very first Saint of the NHS.

ANATHEMA

with acknowledgments to the delectable
Miss Julie Andrews

Comprehensive sixth-formers with well-grown moustaches
Babies with pungent ammonia rashes
Held up too close to my nose and eyelashes
Pop groups with voices less golden than Bing's
These are among my unfavourite things…

Patients who walk in of all creeds and classes
With time on their hands and sit down on their asses
Talking their heads off, unheeding the masses
That seethe in the waiting-room packed like sardines
These are among my unfavourite things…

On the golf-course! In the Algarve!
On the Lido having fun
I keep on remembering my unfavourite things
And then I'm right back to square one!

Domiciliary visits with Geriatricians
Social workers, Case Conferences, Repeat Prescriptions
Sets of dull figures from dull Statisticians
In duller still leaflets that every post brings –
These are my mostest unfavourite things…

A REP REFLECTS

I like to call at Dr Evans's
With gin and tonic for elevenses.

I hate to call at Dr Campbell's –
He spills his coffee on my samples.

I like to call on Dr Bix –
She's 36, 24, 36.

I hate to call at Doc Baumgartner's –
That goes for him and all his partners!

I like to call on Dr Good –
She hasn't but I think she would.

I hate to call on Dr Reith –
They say he choked a Rep to death

I like to call at Dr Bissets –
Some calls on her turn out Night Visits

Dr De Vere I find draconian –
I'm Comprehensive; he's Etonian.

My day's last call, deflated, I'll come
To kind old Dr Burrough's welcome.

PHYSICIANS' POEM[1]

even doctors enjoy versifying about Guinness

This admirable Glow within us
Speaks of Content and also Guinness.
It soothes the Manic, spurs the Sthenic
Reintegrates the Schizophrenic.
A Glass will banish Halitosis
A couple, Onychogryphosis;
Whereas in Baby's feed a dash
Will heal that stubborn Nappy-rash.
Oftimes I've watched, if taken regularly
Guinness diminish Splenomegaly.
Of Disdiadokokinesis
The cure inspired my MD Thesis.
Its use has altered the Prognosis
Times without number in Phimosis,
Unarmed with Guinness, this Condition
More often baffled the Physician.
A Therapeutic Panacea
Most eager to prescribe it we are.

1 This poem was actually used by Guinness in one of their advertisements.

IF THE CAP FITS

I treat my patients chummily, which gains their
adulation
Betimes I use a simile, without equivocation
And as it were caparison for their edification
In garments of comparison my own pontification.

Prolixity's a sin to me, a realm where I don't go at all,
So when my Nurse showed in to me a lady I don't
know at all
And when she begged, 'Explain to me why I'm
lifeless and light-headed,'
I said, 'Here's why – It's plain to me', smiling
kindly as I said it,

'Think of', said I, 'a Merc or Ford, long past first
registration
Whose moving parts don't quite accord, can't pass
a filling-station,
Less than efficient piston-rings, a leaking fuel-system,
Poorly sustained by rusting springs, at least one faulty
piston.

Your chassis, seen from where I sit, might be
described as chequered, marred,
Its brands of fuel down through the years perhaps
two star not super.'
I let my gaze fall on her face and then upon her
Record Card;
Strange how a name befits a case: her name was
Minnie Cooper.

TO MY RECEPTIONIST
MARY FORRESTER

with apologies to Robert Burns

O Mary at thy window be,
   It is the dread Consulting Hour,
These first drops of Humanity
   Do certainly portend a shower
Which, like the rainfed Highland Burn
   Shall surge and swell into a Flood
Imperious and meek in turn,
   Now diffident, now frankly rude.

O Mary of the gentle mien,
   The quiet eye, the helping hand
A trouble-shooter all-supreme
   Among your Sisterhood you stand
And no discourtesies succeed,
   From sufferer or Overlord
In twenty years to change your creed,
'The smile is mightier than the sword.'

Yet, in your nature, not alone
   Compassion lies – there is a spirit
Bred in the mind and in the bone,
   An overtone which you inherit
From earlier heroes – In your blood,
   Leonidas, who held of yore
The Pass: Horatius, Roland good,
   Heroic Katharine – bar-the-door.

The Evening Tide to-day will bear
  A varied and a questing Jetsam
And you will know and you will care
  Just what consoles and what upsets ’em
‘Miss Lion, I am sure you roar,
  Partially deafened though I am,
Mainly because your paw is sore.
  Goodnight, get better soon, Miss Lamb.’

MRS SIDDONS:
CAUTIONARY CASE HISTORY NUMBER 1

Mrs Siddons was prone
When Mr S was playing too much golf
To lifting up her handmaiden the phone,
And crying, 'Wolf!'

Scarce had the magic sound
Ceased its vibration on their tympani,
Than men of healing arts from all around
Rallied in sympathy.

The family doctor, all
Thoughts of slumber lost, expediently,
The surgeon in a domiciliary call
And a Rolls-Bentley.

And the psychiatrist,
Hastening from his bedlam on the hill,
Made answer to her hue and cry and grist
For Mrs Siddons' mill.

Skin specialists forbye
Would leave their wards untended to abet her
Full of that happy breed that never die,
Nor yet get better.

Till once, in middle age.
Outside she ran instead, and as before,
Cried, 'Wolf!' A lithe brown form came
through the hedge,
And more and more.

They made a meal of it,
   Tearing in little fragments Mrs Siddons,
So there remained no recognisable bit –
   And damn good riddance!

MISS LYONS: CAUTIONARY CASE HISTORY NUMBER 2

We very seldom saw Miss Lyons
   (Demure and frail, whose occupation's
A teacher of Domestic Science)
   Excepting for inoculations.

Prior to taking to the seas
   To while away the long vacation
Cruising the Hamadryades
   Or hiking in the Ganges basin,

Or rambling in the Pyrenees
   Or sun-tan seeking in Bermuda
Or walking right round Lake Louise
   Or deep-sea fishing Barracuda.

Protected 'gainst Bubonic Plague
   She walked, indomitable and skinny
Shivering continually with ague
   Right across Papua New Guinea.

And in the summers as I took
   My holidays with my wife's relations
Which didn't call for too much pluck
   I constantly admired my patient's.

We made an excellent team: whilst I
   Strove to afford her full immunity
She ranged the known world far and wide
   Protected from her importunity.

Last year she just went to Torquay
   (With her old mum, a trifle tired),
And after bathing in the sea
   Ran out and suddenly expired.

She made, alas, quite unprotected,
   Early acquaintance with St Peter
I blame myself for I neglected
   Her jellyfish antibody Titre!

MISS BATES:
CAUTIONARY CASE HISTORY NUMBER 3

Passion and kindly old Miss Bates
  My patient up on Solway Ridge
Had never been close stablemates –
  Her only passion was for Bridge

Which, after lunch till close of day
  In turn around each other's houses
Daily and nightly she would play
  With three old like-addicted Pussies.

In one respect her game was flawed
  Her character as well, alas!
She'd bid and bid, but, by the Lord,
  Hardly, if ever, would she *pass*!

The Tuesday before last, at night,
  The second deal – what's this? Oh, Hades!
A not-to-be-forgotten sight
  No more nor less – Eleven spades.

Scarce had she this abundance scanned.
  And thrilled – a vessel wall gave way
And Death himself played out the hand:
  At last she'd passed – she passed away.

NHS SONNET 1

Miss Sims, first of your suffering sisterhood
  To grace my surgery this winter's morn
  Touch you no symptom you cannot adorn!
Have fourteen days sped by since last you stood
Before me? Even-money you'll allude
  To feeling that the power has been and gone
  And left your legs; your tendency to yawn
For half an hour thrice daily after food;
  The constant ringing in your ears (and mine);
  Sensations of inflation in your lung;
Your head, heart, ego, kidney, liver, spine,
  No Sims Component left unwept, unsung!
All is not lost! There's still the Thin Red Line,
  Clean, functional, exuberant … your tongue.

NHS SONNET 2

The vigorous, healthy clatter on my stair
   Heralds the advent of John Henry Brown,
   Who jettisons his fourteen-stone-odd down
Of well-looked-after manhood to declare,
'You'll seldom find me sitting in this chair.'
   A statement so repetitive, I've grown,
   With further fairy-stories of his own,
Ever and ever less inclined to wear.
'I get so bored at home, I'm at a loss,
   And as for staying off work, why I just hate it.
   I think I might feel fit enough if I waited
Until tomorrow…However, you're the Boss,
It's up to you!' Yet, ah indeed, how cross
   He'd be if he left uncertificated.

CHAPTER THIRTEEN

Pot-pourri

The following three longer offerings all have, naturally, a medical connection. The first, *Your Life in Their Hands*, was written for a competition demanding a medical murder mystery. The second, *Dr Nutter's Casebook*, is a revamping of an old legend, whilst the punchline of the third, *Tomlinson,* is a clue to the fact that it was composed in 1979; this piece was runner-up in a literary competition. The two very brief pieces at the end were both runners up in competitions in *Punch* in the mid-sixties: the first competition asked readers to provide a patron saint for a modern phenomenon, the second to compose a song for raising the spirits in World War III – perhaps this should have gone with my comments on the Songs of World Wars I and II – I don't know.

YOUR LIFE IN THEIR HANDS

At the time of the events I am about to relate I was (and still am for that matter) the Senior Partner of a large General Medical Practice, and although perhaps I should not say this, a man of the highest standing in the community. A regular churchgoer, I am regarded as a good listener and so tend to collect in the way of patients more lost dogs a-seeking than my more pragmatic younger partners. I flatter myself that my lack of knowledge of my patients' bodies is more than made up for by my understanding of their minds.

Now, it so happens that every family doctor has one or two patients at least who drive him up the wall. At this point, let me introduce to you Miss Hope (not her real name).

Miss Hope and I have had a relationship (platonic I assure you) for the past 25 years. She regards me as somewhere between the father who left the Hope menage (I was tempted to say nest, but one must eschew the commonplace) early, and the son she never had owing also to her own minus rating in come hither. She is a tallish, rather angular woman, well past the high noon of life with protuberant eyes and recessed neck around which she wears a band of a dark material in the manner of a recently bygone age. Please don't think I am overstressing the physical detractions of Miss Hope which are her misfortune, not her fault. I am merely doing my best to be objective.

To get back to my story, Miss Hope has been in the habit of consulting me, attending my afternoon consulting hour summer and winter, rain or shine for the past 20 years. For 20 minutes approximately, she has delivered herself non-stop of a symptomatology so diverse in content that it would by now easily have filled one of those fat text books of Medicine that adorn my consulting room shelves. This is the way it takes maiden ladies in Miss Hope's case and normally I can take it on the chin, helped I admit by an occasional pot of apple chutney (not that I am struck on apples much) and at Christmas a home-knit pullover of loose texture and sombre appearance.

Let me take you straight forward to the 5 May. There were, I suppose (I realise now) a number of predisposing factors at work in my mind. It was my wedding anniversary for one thing. I had forgotten that it was, and breakfast in consequence had been an even more silent repast than usual. The day before I had missed a two-foot putt on the last green, to be eliminated from the Championship at the Golf Club. That same evening I read verse – I read a good deal of it. The Cavalier Poets I enjoy especially and I feel this underlines the essential gentleness of my nature – but on that night I had taken down the Ancient Mariner and in the magic of Coleridge's words I had revived the tortures of that hapless sailor obsessed by the stare of the ever-watching albatross, until he fetched his crossbow and shot the great bird.

When I greeted my receptionist on my way in to my afternoon consulting hour that day, my smile was as warm as ever but my subconscious was clouded. It was a sunny day as it happened and as I settled down to work I could hear the birds singing in the garden outside and I was beginning almost to enjoy myself when I pressed the buzzer and in walked Miss Hope, folded her wings and began to give tongue.

A thought struck me suddenly. I have ten years to go to retirement. Allowing for five weeks holiday per year that would entail 470 tête-à-têtes with Miss Hope. My spirits quailed. Miss Hope was in full flight and I had switched off as usual when I happened to catch the words 'and my heart races'. I came out of my reverie. 'Lie on the couch', I said. 'There is, a spot on the main artery at the front of the neck called the carotid sinus; pressure on it will control the racing of the heart or slow it down. Let me show you, so that you can do it for yourself in future if necessary.' With hindsight I find it hard to assess my own motives even now – therapeutic or homicidal? Suffice to say that I found myself looking down at the livid features of Miss Hope whose spirit had only too evidently departed the flesh. Furthermore there were marks of pressure to be seen only too clearly on her neck.

I collected my wits. My younger partners may regard my approach to Medicine as rather homespun but my wits at least are as sharp as theirs. I reviewed the situation mentally and the result was less than encouraging. If this goes to a post-mortem, I thought, the Home Office will send up one of their hatchet men and yours truly will be for the high jump.

We live on the premises, my wife and I, and beyond my Consulting Room at the end of the passage is the kitchen door and in between is the door of the Practice Nurse's room. After consulting me, patients are quite prone to spend time with her, so that the Receptionists may well not notice immediately the non-appearance of a given patient. First sticking my head out of the door to make sure that the coast was clear, I shouldered the seven stone of Hermione Hope and I didn't pause till the kitchen door was shut behind me. My wife happened to be spending a few days with her parents who farm, partly in order to bring back meat for the big chest freezer, which was therefore, by the grace of God, currently empty. When I regained my Consulting Room a minute or two later the freezer was full to the brim. I buzzed for the next patient.

That night it so happened that I was on call. The phone rang at 2 a.m., the Buntings' baby with bad croup again. I dressed and went straight out. Miss Hope came with me in the boot. Baby sedated, we drove straight to Miss Hope's ground floor flat. Entry of course was easy, as her front door key was in her handbag.

Fortunately from previous night calls to that same flat I had a good idea where she kept her nightclothes and I had only just got her comfortably in bed, suitably attired, when old Mrs McNulty came pottering in from next door in her dressing gown, wakened by the commotion. I broke the sad news to her as gently as I could and, on a stroke of inspiration, got her to sign a night call form (these enable us to claim a fee for being called out of our beds).

Came the dawn. It found me closeted in my Consulting Room writing out the death certificate with Miss Hope's only surviving relative. This lady told me of her own strong belief in cremation which the deceased had shared. I was pleased to be able to agree that this was my own point of view exactly, and I felt that cremation was at once practical and hygienic. I explained to her that a second certificate from an independent doctor was mandatory.

I rang up old Dr Boyd there and then to do the second certificate. I usually get him to do mine; he retired from Practice twelve years ago on a smallish pension and he greatly appreciates the occasional cremation fee aimed in his direction. In any event when he examines the deceased as he is bound to do by law, he does no more than gingerly lift a corner of the face covering, and he couldn't see much anyway even if he did. I always feel that even if the feathered end of an arrow happened to be protruding from the chest of the departed, it would most probably pass unnoticed by Dr Boyd.

I don't often attend the funeral services of my patients because when one is the Family Doctor one is sometimes conscious of a hint of reproach in the eyes of close relatives, cordial though they may seem, but I did go to Miss Hope's. Very few there, but the Minister made kindly reference to her and I felt myself as I sat listening to him that probably indeed she had been her own worst enemy.

So it has come about that Miss Hope is laid to rest and that I myself am still the well-respected head of a busy Group Practice. When I filled in that part of the cremation certificate where it asks, 'Have you, as far as you know, any pecuniary interest in the death of the deceased?' I could have sworn on the Bible when I wrote the word No.

How was I to know that Miss Hermione Hope was going

to leave me £30,000?

DR NUTTER'S CASEBOOK: AN OLD LEGEND REVAMPED

Husband and wife looked at me in disappointment and disbelief. 'I'm sorry to tell you,' I said, 'the tests have shown that there is no chance of your conceiving a child. I would advise you strongly to consider adoption.'

Some weeks later they were back in my Consulting Room. The adoption societies had held out little hope of a baby in the near or indeed the foreseeable future. These young people, I thought to myself, must have an outlet for their emotions, be it only a surrogate. 'Mr and Mrs Hart,' I said, 'go down to the pet shop in Bank Street and select something furry and four-legged that stands as much in need of affection as yourselves and take it straight home and love and cherish it.'

I lost touch with them for a number of years, then one morning Mr Hart came to consult me alone. He looked strained and older. 'Doctor,' he said, 'have you time to listen to me?' Without waiting for my assent he went straight into his story.

They had gone, he said, straight to the pet shop in Bank Street and made known their wants. The proprietor had listened sympathetically but had shaken his head. 'It so happens,' he said, 'that at this moment I have only guinea pigs and a grass snake which is affectionate without perhaps quite fitting your bill.' Then a thought struck him. 'I have in the back shop,' he said, 'an egg which a traveller has brought me from the Matto Grosso jungle in Brazil. I have no idea of its origin, but he assures me it will hatch in time into a living creature. If you care to have it?'

'Doctor, we were desperate, my wife and I. We took the egg and set it in a warm corner, and we would sit and hold hands and watch it night after night as we waited for it to hatch. This vigil was perhaps the happiest time of our lives. The French have a proverb about travelling hopefully! To my wife that egg was embedded in her womb and I myself felt growing stirrings of impending fatherhood.

'Came the night when my wife greeted me from the office excited and tearful. Without a word she took my hand and led me upstairs. On the spare room bed was a tiny creature such as I had never before clapped eyes on. Bird or mammal I could not say: it had a swan-neck clothed in down, a short body covered in light brown fur, tiny wings, long legs and webbed feet, and, even at that newborn stage, soft brown eyes like Terry Wogan's that looked appealingly up into mine. My wife ran into my arms.

'There began then a time both difficult and delightful – I'm not taking up too much time, Doctor?'

'Of course not,' I said. (I have always stressed the importance of a good history.)

'Feeding was an early problem. No help from Dr Hugh Jolly, and the Vet was little better. After many trials and setbacks when once or twice we feared we had lost him the creature began to thrive and grow bigger on a regular diet of Kelloggs cornflakes and yoghurt and indeed never looked back.

'Then there was the question of what he was. None of the animal-lovers round here could throw any light on the question at all. I wrote eventually to the Museum of Natural History enclosing his most recent photograph, and a long time afterwards they replied. This was a creature last reported in Ecuador three hundred years before and thought to be extinct. It was a Rary!

'This news, we felt, my wife and I, was the sublimation of all our yearnings. We set out to try and match up to the responsibility that Destiny had entrusted to us. The Rary, now tall and slender, was a model pet, well-behaved and attracting admiring glances, not unmixed with curiosity, wherever we went. My wife grew to love him like the son we never had. She would talk to him all day when I was at the office and she felt he could understand every word. For myself, I would take him for long walks along the top of the cliffs in the evenings, always without a lead, for he was biddable and made no attempt to stray.

'But, as sometimes happens in times of great happiness, the horizon clouded. I was so eager to get home at nights that I could not concentrate at the office and in time I lost my job. Money grew tight. I grew irritable with my wife, and, I'm sorry to say, with our Rary. As I grew more withdrawn my wife seemed to spend more and more time with him and I felt shut out and grew jealous. One evening, I'm ashamed to say, I struck her and the Rary put his wings round her and glared angrily at me.

'Things reached a crisis, looking back, when Kelloggs went on strike and there were no cornflakes to be had at all in the supermarkets, and though we stinted ourselves to buy a home yoghurt-maker we watched him growing thinner and knew he wasn't getting enough. Distressed though we both were, we could not bring ourselves to discuss the problem outright. We kept our thoughts to ourselves.

'One morning I opened the *Telegraph*. The FT Index had fallen by 14 points. I came to a decision but said nothing to my wife.

'That evening we set off for our walk, the Rary and I, and walked as usual towards the sunset, which was particularly fine that night. He, who before would walk briskly ahead, now had difficulty in keeping up. We breasted the hill and strolled along the cliffs' top to where they are at their steepest, rising sheet two hundred feet above the ocean. We approached the edge much closer than usual. Something in my manner or my eyes must have alerted the Rary. He stopped me suddenly and spoke.'

' "What are you going to do?" he asked. Astonished, I said to him, "I never knew you could speak."

' "Of course I can speak", he replied, "but nothing that you or your wife has said to date has seemed to call for any comment from me."

' "Well," I said slowly, "it's not that we haven't grown to love you; we have, but maintaining you has become an increasing drain on our resources and I am sorry to say that I have brought you up here to tip you over the cliff into the sea."

'The Rary looked at me with his soft brown eyes like Terry Wogan's and then he looked down at the waves dashing against the foot of the cliff far below.

' "Well," he said, "it's a long way to tip a Rary!" '

TOMLINSON[1]

Now Tomlinson gave up the ghost, not in Berkeley Square but in that modern luxury maisonette he'd just bought with his Unreduced Lump Sum away from the Surgery premises at last. A Spirit came to his bedside and gripped him by the hair, or it would have done if the last of it hadn't fallen out

1 *Pace* Rudyard Kipling

during that complaint of Mrs Todds' to the Medical Service Committee in 1971. The Spirit had to use a fireman's lift instead but it did carry him far away, so that he could distinctly hear the roar of the Milky Way which he identified, the differential diagnosis being the last frustrated wail of his widow or just plain Tinnitus.

Darkness grew light. Peace imbued the air and the doctor's breast. The Spirit led him through some gates, nacreous and shining and his own spirit rose. They entered at length an anteroom with desks where he sat down thankfully, the Spirit remaining at his side. There were others, he saw, seated like himself. An old gentleman with an ineffable sweetness of countenance, gowned as for Surgery, handed out papers, one to each. 'Saint Peter', said the Spirit.

'And these?' The Spirit looked embarrassed. 'Just introduced up here. MCCGP. The Celestial College! A prerequisite! 65% pass mark.'

'My colleagues?' asked Tomlinson, 'Surgeons, physicians, psychiatrists?'

'Later on you may meet Sir Astley Cooper – and Lister.'

'Lord Moran?' the Spirit shook his head sadly. 'As for psychiatrists, there isn't one within a million light years of this place.'

'The price of failure?' asked Tomlinson.

'Put it right out of your mind', said the Spirit. 'That journey's half as long again and I've done it three times this week. I was telling Saint Luke I'll come to a laminectomy yet even if I am disembodied, damned if I won't.

Tomlinson had grown thirstier since leaving the Earth's atmosphere. 'I wonder', he said, 'a small glass of nectar?' The Spirit shook his head regretfully. 'Not unless', he said. Tomlinson resigned himself (GPs are seldom short on resignation), picked up a gold pen marked CIBA 18 carat and gave attention to the paper in front of him. He was surprised to read the legend at the top. 'This paper is supplied by Celestos the elite Beta Blocker – normal rhythm quickly restored after irregularities or tachycardia due to excessive bliss.' He looked at the Spirit who shrugged his shoulders. 'The perfect life has to be paid for you know.'

He addressed himself to the paper, which began:

1. Are you:
(a) A True Believer?
(b) An Atheist?
(c) An Agnostic?
Tick the appropriate answer

Tomlinson, as a General Practitioner had told as many lies as most, but he sensed that he was on oath as it were, though no one had told him. He ticked Agnostic but put in brackets:

> a reverent agnostic like Professor Gilbert Murray.

2. Why?

Tomlinson reflected and then wrote:

> Because the world is full of innocent and endearing creatures, animals be they wild or experimental, children perhaps who suffer savage fates at the hands of their more highly developed homologues. The True Believer doesn't raise his head from his devotions long enough to bestow on them more than a cursory glance.

The next two questions seemed to follow from his answers to Question 2, although Tomlinson didn't really notice. Perhaps he was tired.

3. Have you made much noise about this in your time?

> No – very little.

4. *Are you a Vegetarian?*

   No.

Then on another tack:

5. *Have you ever struck:*
   - *(a) A patient?*
   - *(b) An administrator?*
   - *(c) An orthopaedic surgeon?*
   - *(d) A health visitor?*

After reflection, Tomlinson answered ‘No’ to each. As it happened, his wife had her Health Visitor’s Certificate but he deemed, correctly, that the questions were posed in the purely professional sense.

6. *Define Primary Care.*

This again wasn’t easy to answer as he had himself wondered many a time what the words meant. The son of a General Practitioner whose father had taken pride in looking after his patients from cradle to grave, he had striven to follow the parental example. He wrote eventually:

> I do not feel qualified to answer this question. I was due to go on a course once in Primary Care at the College of General Practitioners, but I couldn’t get a Locum at the last minute and didn’t make it.

7. *Did you love your patients:*

(a) Not much?
(b) A good deal?
(c) Too much?

Another tricky one. A very decent bunch on the whole, with a few exceptions that drove him into the ground, but on the other tack there was that affair in 1954 with Mrs Sanderson who told him he looked like Lew Ayres. Rather quickly he ticked, 'A good deal'.

8. *Give four reasons why you should be admitted to membership.*
   (1) I have for thirty-three years worn a hair shirt called Mrs Robinson-Smythe.
   (2) I am patient with Social Workers. I have even attended case conferences.
   (3) In 1965 Mrs O'Reilly came in one morning and said, 'If ever there was a Saint, Doctor Tomlinson, it's yourself.'
   (4) I like a good glass of nectar.

9. *How does your mind conceive the Celestial Health Service? (Be brief – tautology is not esteemed in Heaven.)*

Tomlinson composed in his mind a short pastiche and then filleted it:

- Fewer forms (no temporary residents up here).
- An autocratic institution taking its nod from the All-Highest. [A vague impression of 14, Princes Gate, Hyde Park, HQ of the College of GPs, entered his mind and as quickly left it.]
- Euphoria on all sides, perhaps requiring sedation (hard to contemplate life without Valium, even in Paradise).
- An excess of self-esteem in some cases (one has a good deal of experience in treating patients with this distressing condition, all without exception confident of salvation).

And finally:

10. *Were you a good doctor?*

Tomlinson pondered this long indeed. So much, he felt,

depended. The question was open to a dichotomy of interpretation. A man might for instance be a good politician and yet be the antithesis of a 'good' politician. At length he wrote, 'God alone knows!' folded the paper and handed it in.

There was an interval. Tea was served. Spiritual music from an unseen orchestra rose in a soft voluptuous swell. Hours passed that seemed like aeons. Tomlinson passed the time of day with his neighbour, an angular nonconformist who hadn't been any too pleased with his funeral arrangements.

A door opened and into a room suddenly suffused with light there entered a tall shining figure. 'The Archangel Michael', whispered the Spirit, shimmying to his feet. The Archangel came straight to Tomlinson, hand outstretched. 'Congratulations! But your doctoring days are over. Welcome to the CDC – our own Celestial Diplomatic Corps.' He held up Tomlinson's exam paper and waved it in approval. 'My son,' he said, 'you've done a David Owen!'

❁ ❁ ❁

These final two pieces were both published in *Punch*

A PATRON SAINT FOR A MODERN PHENOMENON

Son of a poor woman, the Widow Goody, his childhood was spent in Renaissance Liverpool. A passion for discipline, early manifest, irked his schoolfellows, who tore off his fingernails. He journeyed the length of the land, preaching order. In Sunderland angry serfs pursued him, hurling empty mead flagons. The Anfield Riots cost him an eye. Bemaddened Burghers of Bristol bit off an ear. Broken on the wheel of Spion Kop his untimely death followed in his native town. His entrails were fed to dogs. His flayed body hung a twelvemonth before the Moot Hall in Oldham. Canonised in 1832, Saint Goodison became Patron Saint of the Association of Football Referees in 1921.

A SONG TO RAISE SPIRITS IN WORLD WAR III

Past the second Forte's where the Motorway
Strides across the Hillside at the close of day,
Bright as of Yore, your Eyes, it seems,
Transcend in Dreams, the Headlamps' Beams.
  My Lily of the Laybys,
  My own Lili Marlene.

Out in Okinawa, back where I came in,
Still I see you waiting by the Litter-bin.
Here, where the Fall-out falls like Rain,
For You I'd fain, fall out again,
  My Lily of the Laybys
  My own Lili Marlene.

CHAPTER FOURTEEN

Oz

I thought it would be pleasant to round off this miscellany in a warmer climate – Australia. This vast continent is impressive for much more than simply its sheer size. It also has a wonderful variety of scenery, ranging from a few primal rain forests to an area which could well be mistaken for our Lake District, and there is of course space galore in town and country. I have tried to play fair in this book and to relate everything about which I have written either to myself or my family and their doings, or to Carlisle and its citizens and their doings. I feel that it is likewise possible to justify my Australian reminiscences on two counts.

So my first justification for writing about Australia is that our son, Hugh, has practised as a Psychiatrist in that country for the past twenty years, and we have managed to visit every second year in January, which is high summer there. Our Australian daughter-in-law, Helen, is reservations manageress in Sydney for Thai Airways and in consequence we have travelled the last four times by that airline which is very comfortable and efficient and has the added attraction that Thai air-hostesses are the most beautiful of all and gently solicitous of one's well-being. Although the journey by air will always take at least 24 hours, earlier flights involved two stops to change planes, but more recently only one stop has become necessary, in Bangkok.

Hugh has worked for some years now in Sydney, which can be very hot, but a tongue of the harbour seems to reach practically every suburb of the city, making for coolness. We have had experience of two other towns besides Sydney. Firstly, we twice visited Orange when Hugh was working there in a large District Mental Hospital. At first sight the main street in Orange might suggest an American frontier town of the Wild West, and indeed it is probably thought of as an outback town since it lies about 150 miles west of Sydney. The facilities there, however, are far from outback standard. Orange boasts two championship golf courses, an Olympic-size swimming pool and a civic centre where a large mobile orchestra pit moves up and down mechanically. Just to confuse the visitor, there are billboards everywhere announcing 'Orange is Apple Country.' The streets of these smaller outback towns like Whitehaven and Silloth are wide and laid out at right angles in the characteristic colonial pattern.

In due course Hugh moved 35 miles nearer Sydney, to the provincial university town of the area, Bathurst, which possesses two cathedrals, no less. To reach these towns from Sydney one passes through the spectacular Blue Mountains, climbing gradually to 3,000 ft. Orange and Bathurst lie on the plain above so in summer the climate is pleasantly cooler. It is interesting to reflect that it wasn't until 1852 that they succeeded in pushing roads through the Blue Mountains and reaching these areas which were therefore not developed until the mid-nineteenth century.

I said I felt justified in including my Australian impressions in this book on two counts. The second count is in connection with Ayers Rock, the famous tourist attraction which some of my readers may even have visited, although I haven't actually been there myself and which has, it seems a strong Carlisle connection. I discovered not long ago that Ayers Rock took its name from a Carlisle citizen whose descendant was a patient of mine, the late Donald Ayers – known and respected in this city as a city councillor, Scout Commissioner and Magistrate. You will remember that Ayers Rock was the scene a number of years ago of a murder case that made headlines around the world – the so-called Dingo Murder – the dingo being the wild dog of Australia. It was alleged at the time that the baby who died was carried off by a dingo. My son Hugh was very marginally involved in this case having been asked at one stage to give a professional opinion on the mental condition of the mother. As far as I remember the two accused were convicted of murdering the baby and then freed a number of years later when fresh evidence came to light, but I can't be too certain of this.

Although we have travelled extensively in New South Wales and in Queensland we have never been west of these, although they are big enough in all conscience. Wherever one travels, one comes across refreshing differences from the UK. For instance, some years back in Port McQuarie, a charming seaside resort 400 miles north of Sydney, we found that the sea birds – in large numbers – were pelicans. In addition there was a holiday camp beside the harbour, which, at 10 a.m. prompt every morning, would discharge through a pipe a large quantity of fish refuse. At 9.45 a.m. the pelicans would form a queue, an example in orderliness to their human counterparts and wait patiently for their breakfast.

Also in Port McQuarie is a church of great interest: brick-built by convicts and dating from the beginning of the nineteenth century it is in splendid order despite being one of the oldest buildings in that very new country. Furthermore, apparently there was then nothing with which to make cement, but since oysters abounded on the harbour wall (they still do), the shells were ground down to provide all the cement.

McQuarie, from whom the resort takes its name, is the most illustrious name in New South Wales. Lachlan McQuarie left the Hebridean island of Benbecula as a youngster in the early nineteenth century, to make a career in Australia at a time when it was still peopled mostly by transported convicts. In 1806 he became Governor of New South Wales, succeeding the celebrated Captain Bligh, and was probably unique in that he worked constantly for the well-being of the convicts and was fair and incorruptible. His name crops up all over New South Wales: McQuarie Street in Sydney, McQuarie River, Lady McQuarie Point in Sydney and even a Loch McQuarie.

In fact it is probably true to say that in Australia, despite its policy in recent years of admitting all races fairly equally, British names still predominate and British ways are pretty widespread as well, perhaps not surprisingly seeing that the Australians do talk fairly straight Cockney don't they? To give another example of British place names: about fifteen years ago we paid a delightful visit to the Barrier Reef (Great Keppel Island). The other islands include Carlisle Island with Brampton Island right beside it, and the Cumbrians were obviously a force to be reckoned with early on as you will find a satellite town of Sydney called Penrith. The Barrier Reef itself is heaven but, like most earthly paradises these days, it's getting pretty expensive to visit.

More British names can be found about three hours' drive south of Sydney where there is a large and beautiful bay, called Jervis Bay, home to the main Australian Naval Base, a lovely area which we have visited more than once, and which also has a town called Vincentia. This all commemorates the

Battle of Cape St Vincent, on the glorious 1 June, where Admiral Sir John Jervis defeated the French and was created Earl St Vincent.

And the Australians themselves? A visitor once described Australians slightly disparagingly as 'a race of middle-aged men in shorts, wedded to their barbies.' Perhaps he has a point, yet both shorts and barbecues have their virtues and advantages. Professional men such as lawyers can often be seen wearing shorts in the business section of Sydney and these, with shirt and tie and, particularly, knee-length stockings rather than socks, look perfectly smart and are of course much more appropriate to the climate than business suits. As for the barbecues, in 'Oz' dinner or supper is usually eaten *al fresco* and is invariably cooked by Father who develops a proprietary right to the barbecue, thus taking the burden from Mum, which she quite appreciates. The barbecue habit has probably given rise to the often-heard expression, deprecating mental capacity, 'one banger short of a barbie'.

Australians are wonderfully hospitable in their own country and there is none of the residual class-consciousness still prevailing in the UK. In Australia Jack has always been as good as his master, something I myself noted long before I had any inkling that I would one day be a regular visitor to the country. During the war, I remember being attached to the Australian Ninth Division for a week in the desert and travelling once in their Colonel's car where I heard him addressed by his driver as Jack. If I had dared to call my then CO Ernest, I should have been on the next boat home!

You could say Australians have it all: their wines are pretty wonderful too! And even Australian bees don't sting!